Narrative Therapy with Children and their Families

by Michael White and Alice Morgan

DULWICH CENTRE PUBLICATIONS
Adelaide, South Australia

ISBN 0 9752180 2 6

Cover Artwork:
Anna Waters (7 years)
Ben Rate (8½ years)

Proof Reading:
Jane Hales and Anne Prior

Published by
Dulwich Centre Publications
Hutt St PO Box 7192
Adelaide 5000, South Australia
P: (61-8) 8223 3966
E: dcp@dulwichcentre.com.au • W: www.dulwichcentre.com.au

Contents

Introduction

by Alice Morgan

Welcome to this book about narrative therapy with children and their families! It is delightful for Michael and me to be sharing some stories of therapeutic work with you. This book contains various ideas and practices that we have found to be helpful in assisting children and families to join together in the face of the predicaments for which they seek help and to provide some relief from these predicaments.

This book has been written for all those who have contact with children and families and who wish to enable particular conversations that can contribute to building communities for children that value their skills, knowledges, beliefs, abilities and preferences. We know of teachers, community workers, therapists, youth workers, parents, caregivers of children, child protection workers, school staff and health professionals who use narrative ideas to inform their responses to children. We hope the writings here are relevant to your lives and work and to the lives of the children with whom you are connected.

Two key elements – ideas and skills

This book combines two key elements: 1) stories and detailed examples of therapeutic work with children and their families, and 2) an examination of the ideas and principles that inform this work.

We hope these two elements are combined in such a way that is both practical and relevant. In all the chapters, the 'how to' (or the skills associated with narrative practice) interweave with the ideas that inform those practices (or the why of what we are doing).

For many years I was fortunate to work with children and their families in a range of different contexts: in schools, in community-based organisations, in independent practice and in group contexts. Each context provided me, as a therapist, with different challenges, dilemmas, joys, struggles, complexities and inspirations. As this book has been taking shape, I've recalled the faces of so many different children and their sisters, brothers, parents, friends, grandparents, pets and toys and so on! I can remember many tender conversations and looks of pride and relief as difficulties were addressed.

I can also think of times in conversations when things did not go so well, when either my understanding of narrative ideas, or my ability to engage with narrative skills led to dead-ends. When this happened, I noticed some of the effects it had on me and the families with whom I was meeting. These times invited me into thoughts of 'this isn't working', to places of feeling stuck or constricted, to experiencing the work as having very limited options, and to experiences of 'hopelessness' as a therapist. These were places that were a long way from my preferences for my work! What helped at these times was to revisit the guiding ideas informing narrative practice, and also to revisit and re-engage with the particular conversational and questioning skills that are a narrative therapists' 'tools of the trade'.

It is with this in mind that this book has been published. It is hoped that the chapters here will stretch both thinking and practice. It is hoped that focusing on both the ideas and skills of narrative practice will support practitioners who are working with children and their families.

A focus on micro-maps and skills

The chapters of this book contain examples and explanations of some of the micro-maps of narrative practice that have been developed by Michael White. These include: externalising conversations (Chapter 1), re-membering conversations (Chapter 3), scaffolding conversations (Chapter 1), outsider-witness practices and definitional ceremony (Chapter 4), and re-authoring conversations (Chapters 2, 4 & 5).

Broader considerations – the ideas informing the work

Throughout the book we have also drawn attention to a range of broader considerations and to the thinking that informs narrative practice with children and their families. For instance, the contributions of Barbara Myerhoff, Lev Vygotsky and others are examined. We have included discussions about certain important distinctions and their implications for therapeutic practice. For example, in Chapter 3, Michael White clarifies distinctions between eliciting double-storied accounts of trauma and those forms of therapeutic inquiry based on modern notions of catharsis. In Chapter 5, in an interview relating to collaborative practices, Michael refers to the modern-day eugenics agenda and its effect on child protection investigations. In Chapter 4, I discuss identity as a social, relational and collaborative project (as distinct from identity being innate, internal and unchanging). While Chapter 2 discusses the different ways a therapist can position themselves in conversations with children and their families in order to make it easier to examine the effects of these differing positions on the lives of those consulting us.

Complexities and Dilemmas

There is, however, much more to this book than just these two principle elements. Many other themes and questions are addressed in the papers and interviews. Attention is given to a range of specific complexities and dilemmas related to work with children and their families. Here are just a few examples of the sorts of questions that chapters in this book address:

- What if people report the problem is getting worse or bigger? (Chapter 2)
- How can I work with children who have experienced trauma in ways that are not re-traumatising of them? (Chapter 3)
- What do I do when, for example, I feel myself getting into a position of

convincing children or adults that a development is in fact a development? Alternatively, how do I respond if the young person says, for example: 'That's no big deal, I wish you'd stop going on about it?' (Chapter 2)

- How can I work with other family members present? How can I involve interested people to support the work'? (Chapters 2, 4 & 5)
- What if people can't attend face-to-face meetings? Are there other ways to involve them? (Chapter 4)
- In what ways can I thicken accounts of children's skills and knowledges? (All Chapters)
- What can I keep in mind, in meetings with children and their parents, when their communication is filled with expressions of conflict and misunderstanding? (Chapter 5)
- When I hear of possible 'unique outcomes' or 'exceptions' to the dominant problem-saturated story, what options are there for inquiry that will contribute to rich story development? (Chapter 1 & 4)
- How can I avoid circumstances for conversations to descend into parental complaint and then children's denial and then further complaint, and so on ... how can this be avoided? (Chapter 5)
- How are collaborative practices relevant within child-protection investigations? (Chapter 5)
- If people don't see eye-to-eye on what the problem is, what then? (Chapters 2 & 5)

Special responsibilities of therapists

Some of the particular responsibilities of therapists in relation to work with children and their families are also discussed in this book. These include, but are in no way limited to, the following responsibilities:

- to pay attention to relations of power;
- to prioritise children's safety;
- to structure conversations that do not contribute to re-traumatising children;

- to unpack or deconstruct dominant discourses of local culture, e.g. mother-blaming, individualism, heterosexual dominance, notions of 'normality', and so on;
- to provide contexts whereby multi-storied accounts of life and relationships are celebrated and embraced;
- to co-author conversations to bring forward and thicken children's preferred stories of identity;
- to provide contexts that make collaboration more possible between family members who are in dispute;
- to establish conditions that are conducive for the development of personal agency for those who consult us.

Conclusion

The stories in the pages ahead question normalising notions of identity and relationships. The work illustrated here describes ways in which adults and children can join together around shared commitments and beliefs in order to address the predicaments they may be facing. We hope you enjoy this collection, and that it stimulates, invigorates and supports the work you are doing with children and their families.

Happy reading!

CHAPTER ONE

Narrative Practice with Families with Children: Externalising conversations revisited

by Michael White

Introduction

In this chapter, I will review developments in my work with families with young children over more than twenty years. Looking back at this work over this period will provide an opportunity to revisit the development of a range of narrative practices, including externalising conversations. I will share three stories of work with young children and their families, and then chart the therapeutic conversations associated with these three stories onto three maps of narrative practice. The first map I refer to as a 'statement of position map, version 1'. Over the last decade I have taken recourse to this 'statement of position map' in order to unpack externalising practices in teaching contexts, and to describe the preliminary steps in the sort of rich story development that is founded upon 'unique outcomes' or 'exceptions'. The second map that I will describe in this paper is a 'statement of position map, version 2.' This second version of this statement of position map provides a guide to therapists in rendering the unique outcomes/exceptions of people's lives highly significant. The third map that I will describe here is a 'scaffolding conversations map'. In recent years, I have been utilising this scaffolding conversations map to provide a second description of a range of narrative practices. In the development of this scaffolding conversations map I was inspired by the work of the Russian psychologist, Lev Vygotsky.

So, let me begin by introducing you to the stories of my work with three children: Richard, Gerry and Millie, and their families.

Richard

Richard is a boy of seven years of age who was brought to see me by his sole parent mother, Jane. Richard wasn't doing well in life. He was generally fearful, quite frail, considered to be 'school phobic', and was suffering from a condition that was believed to be 'psychosomatic'. As well as this, he was experiencing persistent insomnia. Richard's father had abandoned the family when he was an infant, and from that time had no contact with Richard.

In response to my questions about Richard's experiences of life, I learned that he'd had some experiences of trauma which were not recent, and I consulted Jane about her thoughts on the merits of addressing this in the context of our therapeutic conversations. Jane said that she thought that it might be a good idea to attend to these experiences, but wondered if there was something that I could do that might have a more immediate effect on Richard' fearfulness, which was becoming increasingly pervasive. In witnessing the present circumstances of Richard's life, this was a priority that I could highly appreciate.

To attend to this priority, I encouraged Richard to introduce me to these fears that were giving him such a hard time – I wanted him to characterise these fears for me so that I would have some idea of what he was up against. He was surprised by this request, and there was suddenly a spark of interest in his eyes. We soon decided that I might get a better picture of things if he painted his fears. I fetched some art materials, and Richard went to work. I peered over his shoulder as he did so, and as these fears began to take shape it took my breath away to see what Richard had been struggling with. These were indeed very scary fears, and I observed:

M: No-one who had fears like this running around in their lives would be able to get any sleep at all!

Richard: Well, I hardly get any sleep myself!

M: Well, is that fair?

Richard: What?

M: Do you think it is fair that these fears take away your sleep?

Richard: No, it's not fair. It's really not fair.

M: Are the neighbors getting any sleep with these fears on the loose at night?

Richard: Uh.

M: Are the neighbors ...

Richard: What do you think mum?

Jane: Maybe you could ask them?

Richard: Okay, I'll do it! I'll do it as soon as I get home. Mum, I'll ask Mrs Murphy first. And then I could go and see Johnny and find out what is happening there.

M: Has Johnny been looking tired lately?

Richard: Has he mum?

I invited Richard to take a further step in characterising these fears by naming them, and we then spent some time figuring out what these fears were up to in his life, and what this said about the agenda of these fears. It didn't take long for us to develop some understanding of the specific tactics employed by these fears to set themselves up as an authority in Richard's life, of the purposes that shaped these tactics, and of the plans that these fears had for his future.

As all of this became clearer to Richard, he became quite indignant and decided that he wasn't all that happy about going along with the plans that the fears had dreamt up for his life. In fact, this suddenly seemed quite intolerable to him. The three of us then spent some time figuring out why it was that he was so displeased with these fear-filled plans for his future, and before long we were discovering what it was that he wanted for his life that didn't fit with the agenda of the fears.

It was upon this basis that Richard decided that some action would just have to be taken:

Richard: Something just has to be done about this.

M: Sorry, what …?

Richard: Something just has to be done about this. These fears need a good education.

M: Oh, so a good education would …

Richard: Fix things, yeah …

M: Okay. Great!

As our conversation unfolded I learned that Richard was going to begin by educating his fears about what he wanted for his life, about his own plans for his future. What's more, he decided that these fears shouldn't be free to roam about at night creating havoc in his life and in his connections with others. To this end, he developed a program to curtail their activities:

Richard: These fears could be upsetting everyone.

M: Yeah, they could be.

Richard: They must be ruining other people's sleep.

M: Probably.

Richard: They shouldn't be allowed just to run around all over the place at night.

M: I reckon you could be right about that.

Richard: They should be locked up at night.

M: Locked up at night?

Richard: Yeah.

M: How would you do this?

Richard: I'll put them in a box and tie it up.

M: Sounds like a good plan. When will you do this?

Richard: Before bedtime.

M: What then? Will you just keep them tied up in a box all of the time?

Richard: No, I'll let them free in the morning before school, so that they can just play around.

M: This does sound like a good plan!

Jane: It sure does.

When we met again three weeks later, I learned that, with Jane's support, Richard had put these plans to educate his fears and to curtail their activities into action. He had brought back to this meeting the paintings that he'd done of his fears. This time they were shut safely in a cardboard box, which was secured by strong elastic. Richard had been feeling much better, and as a consequence of this had been sleeping more soundly and had returned to school on a part-time basis. He was looking stronger and more confident. Upon hearing about the initiatives and efforts that Richard had undertaken to educate the fears and to curtail their activities, I asked about how the fears had taken this. Richard informed me that it hadn't been easy for the fears, and that 'they had been quite pesky'. He then demonstrated this peskiness:

Richard: Look, they wriggle a lot. They wriggle a lot. (The box clearly shaking in his hands.)

M: Yes I can see that. But I can see that when you've got hold of them they don't wriggle too much, do they.

Richard: No, they don't wriggle too much.

M: Let's see if they wriggle when I've got hold of them.

Richard: Okay. (Richard passes the box to Michael.)

M: Oh. Oh. (As Michael takes the box the fears begin to wriggle a lot.)

Richard: Be careful.

M: Oh. Oh. Oh. (The situation is deteriorating, and now the fears are jolting Michael around in his chair.)

Richard: Look out!

M: Oh. Oh. Oh. (Michael is now being gyrated around in his chair by the fears, and is barely able to keep hold of the box.)

Richard: Watch out, watch out!

M: Oh. Oh. Help! Help! (Michael is thrown to the floor, the gyrations have now increased in amplitude, and he fears that the box will get free of his grasp.)

Richard: I've got it! (Richard leaps out of his chair and seizes the box, saving Michael from a terrible fate.)

M: Phew! That was close! So close! Oh thanks, thanks. (Clearly shaken up,

Michael rather unsteadily pulls himself back onto this chair, and tries to get himself together again.)

Jane: Hey look. Look, they tried to get out!

Richard: (Standing beside his chair, with the box on his seat, looking very proud of himself on account of the intervention he'd made into a situation that was looking pretty grim.) Yeah. See here's the flying one sticking out, and here's the creepy-crawly one sticking out too.

M: (Still breathing heavily and looking quite disheveled.) Oh boy, it is lucky that you were here.

The steps that Richard took to educate his fears and to curtail their activities worked out very well for him, and over a period of weeks he achieved a fear-free life. On account of this achievement, he was awarded a 'Fear Busting and Monster Taming Certificate', and was granted membership of the 'Fear Busters and Monster Tamers Society of Australia and New Zealand' (in the early 1980s this was quite an active society with a wide membership). Richard decided to take this certificate to school to show his peers in the hope of identifying another child who was a member of this same very secret society. Although his peers showed considerable interest in this certificate and were curious to hear about the story behind it, he was unsuccessful in his efforts to find other members of the society, except for one small girl who thought she might have been a member earlier in the history of her life.

One unexpected outcome of showing this certificate to his peers, and of his sharing of the story of the fear-taming exploits that it symbolised, was that several other children felt emboldened to speak to Richard about what is not routinely spoken of in the context of the culture of the schoolyard – these children began to speak about their own fears and insecurities. In response to this, Richard suggested that these children give him their fears to tame, with the agreement that he would return these fears to them when it was safe for them to have them back. So, for a time, Richard became an unofficial school counsellor. Later, he was appointed President of the 'Fear Busters and Monster Tamers Society of Australia and New Zealand'. This society flourished under his tenure.

Discussion

My work with Richard and Jane was shaped by what I have referred to in more recent years as a 'statement of position map, version 1.' (This map represents my efforts to unpack externalising practices). I will trace this conversation here, placing in parentheses the specific categories of inquiry around which this map is constructed.

My conversations with Richard and Jane were structured around four general stages. First, I invited Richard to characterise the fears through the painting and the naming of them ('negotiating an experience – near and particular definition of the problem'). Second, together we drew out an account of what the fears were up to, with a significant focus on the consequences of their activities ('mapping of the effects of the problem's activities'). Third, I encouraged Richard to evaluate these consequences and, in response to this, he expressed his displeasure and indignation – he was clearly not happy about going along with these ('evaluating the effects of the problems activities'). Fourth, I requested that Richard, with his mother's assistance, help me to understand why it was that he was so displeased with, and so indignant about, the consequences of the fears' activities ('justifying the evaluation'). At this stage, Richard had the opportunity to identify what it was that he wanted for his own life, and to articulate some of the purposes and plans associated with this.

Although our conversation did not evolve through these four stages in a strictly linear fashion – it did not move smoothly through stages one to four – it was of a progressive nature. In the first place, the problem which had come to characterise Richard, defining his existence and his sense of self, was in itself characterised. And, finally, we were engaged in a conversation in which Richard's identity was being newly characterised in terms of specific aspirations, purposes and plans for his own life. This provided him with a foundation to define actions that he might take to reclaim his life from the fears, actions that were in harmony with what we had all been learning about these aspirations, purposes and plans.

Figure one provides an illustration of the charting of my initial conversation with Richard and Jane.

Figure 1

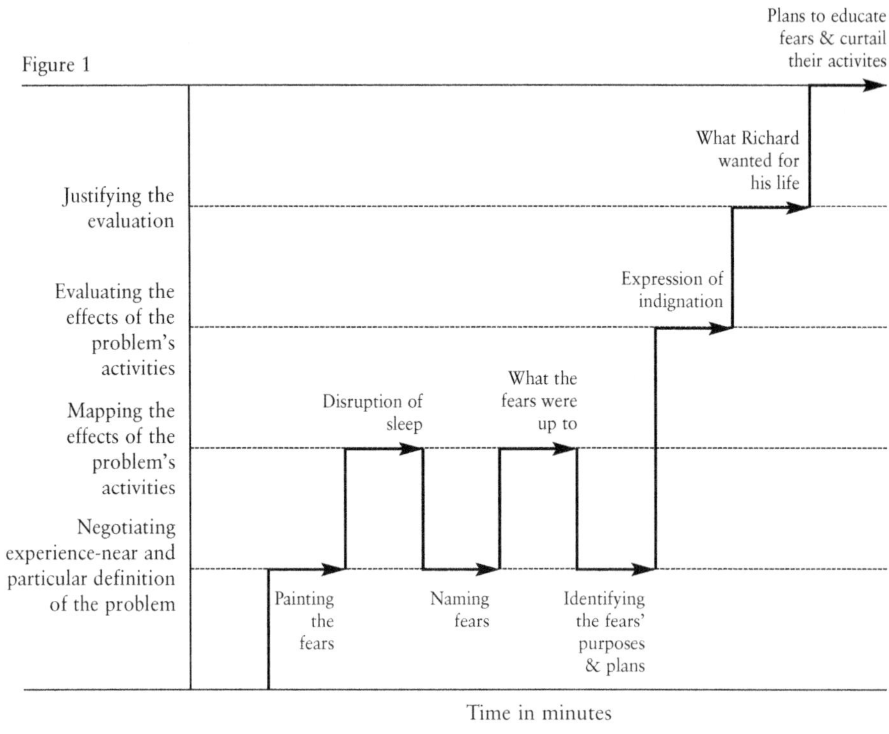

Comment

At times, other therapists have taken the idea of externalising conversations to be a proposal that we assist people to do battle with the problems of their lives, in order to either defeat and vanquish these problems, or to banish them. However, this has not been my understanding about the nature of these conversations. I recently undertook a review of the articles I'd written over the past twenty or so years on the subject of externalising to discover that in just one of these had I presented battle and contest metaphors. Those metaphors that feature much more prominently in the history of my writing about this subject are geological metaphors through which people engage in acts of 'reclaiming' their lives and of 'undermining' problems, political metaphors of 'protest' and 'resistance', liberation metaphors of 'freedom' and 'escape', geographical metaphors of 'gaining ground' and 'recovering territory', educational metaphors of 'teaching' and 'supervision', metaphors of light such as 'overshadowing' and 'enlightening' the problem, and so on.

Although these metaphors have mostly been drawn from the expressions of people seeking counselling, I have played a significant role in the selection of these. For example, a child might be reporting on his/her new initiatives to resolve his/her encopresis (soiling), providing an account of how s/he is now 'beating Mr Mischief' (competition metaphor) with the intention of 'getting my life back from Mr Mischief' (reclamation metaphor). In such circumstances it would be common for me to emphasise the reclamation metaphor in my questions when inviting the child to draw out these initiatives. This selection is based on a concern about the consequences of routinely reproducing battle, contest and/or competition metaphors in the context of therapeutic conversations.

It is significant to note that Richard never set out to vanquish his fears. Instead, his approach was benevolent. He was quite firm in his resolve to educate and enlighten these fears about how they might do what was in his best interests, and in the best interests of other children.

Gerry

Gerry, four years of age, was a pale, thin and short boy, who'd had a life-threatening gastro/intestinal illness in his first year of life. He was hospitalised on account of this illness, and for a period of time he was treated in an intensive care unit. As a consequence of the nature of this illness and the suffering associated with the treatment of it, which included a significant separation from his parents, from thereon Gerry associated the consumption of food and fluids with trauma and with nausea. He became food phobic and a very picky eater.

Over the next few years, the concerted efforts on behalf of his parents, his pediatrician and hospital staff to address this predicament were to no avail – he failed to thrive. Gerry's pediatrician was now very concerned about his growth hormone levels, and referred this family to me in the hope that a 'fresh approach' might be effective in modifying Gerry's orientation to food.

In my first meeting with Gerry and his parents I encouraged them to characterise the 'eating problem'. His parents understood this problem to be a 'phobia', and Gerry was familiar with this name even though he didn't know what it meant. I asked the parents to describe this phobia in terms that would be understood by Gerry, and very soon he was willingly participating in a conversation about what the 'very naughty little phobia' was up to.

Following this, I joined with family members in an exploration of the multiplicity of ways that this phobia was affecting their lives and their relationships with each other, and with the outside world. For the parents, this naughty little phobia, apart from other things, constantly demanded their attention, interfered with their parenting, and contributed to very significant frustration on a day-to-day basis in their efforts to ensure their son's wellbeing. And for Gerry, apart from other things, it became clear that this phobia excluded him from so many activities that he longed to engage in, like climbing trees, playing with his peers, riding a bike, and going fishing with his grandfather. Going fishing with his grandfather, as his cousins did, was something that he longed to do, but he was too frail to hold a fishing rod.

As the meeting unfolded, I learned more about these frustrated longings by encouraging Gerry and his parents to describe the activities that he would be free to engage in if it wasn't for the influence of this phobia. I then asked them to characterise the sort of strength that would be required to prevail against this phobia and to undertake these highly valued activities. Before long, Gerry determined that this would have to be the strength of a tiger – 'tiger strength'*. Gerry was clearly enthusiastic about getting some of this tiger strength for his own life, and this provided an opportunity to introduce a

---

* In the mid-eighties I was meeting with a number of families with children who had 'eating problems', and it was interesting just how often these children chose the tiger metaphor in the characterisation of this strength – although there was the occasional appearance of Tasmanian Devils and Rhinos. Today, early in the 21st century, it seems that tigers do not have such an exalted place in children's culture, and other metaphors are more commonly chosen.

conversation about where he might find a tiger to welcome into his life, and about what would be necessary to sustain the strength of this tiger. Of course, as you could guess, this turned the focus of our attention to tiger diets and the eating habits of tigers, and to general observations about their extraordinary constitution – including the fact that tigers can eat virtually anything and never get sick or even suffer from nausea. When I remarked that most children knew this about tigers, Gerry quickly pronounced that this was a fact that he had known all the way along.

We were soon putting together a menu of the sort of foods and fluids that regularly feature in tiger diets. Gerry took the lead in this, proclaiming foods and fluids like fruit loops, oranges, beetroot, and milkshakes to be regular tiger fare. And we were also soon talking more about what Gerry's life would look like when his tiger was present, and when he was drawing upon tiger strength to do the things that he wanted to do in life. At this juncture, Gerry's mother informed me that her own mother was a dressmaker by trade, and that she would be only too happy to put together a tiger suit in exactly Gerry's proportions.

Then we worked out a deal that instantaneously made Gerry happy, but that initially provoked not insubstantial anxiety in his parents. In fact, they seemed to go through what could only have been momentary panic. This was the deal: from the moment that Gerry recruited a tiger into his life he would no longer be required to eat for himself. Instead he would have to be prepared to stand aside to let his tiger feed. His tiger would henceforth sit in for him at all mealtimes in the family home. As Gerry's parents began to realise that this was a proposal for Gerry to visit the dinner table in the tiger costume, and for him to stand aside at this time to let his tiger feed, their panic dissipated, they grinned broadly and visibly relaxed.

The family went away from my meeting with a plan to visit the Adelaide Zoo to meet the local tigers, and to photograph them. They also agreed to join Gerry in the development of a tiger album, which would include the tiger menu, a story about the arrival of this tiger in Gerry's life, and a story about his agreement to stand aside to let his tiger feed. There was a plan to further develop this album through the inclusion of all sorts of tiger paraphernalia, and for the parents to review this with Gerry each evening at bedtime.

At the very next meeting, three weeks later, I learned that Gerry's tiger had already begun to develop a healthier appetite – apart from other things, he had been eating beetroot and oranges for the first time. At my request, Gerry led me through a review of the beautiful tiger album that he and his parents had been developing, and I seized upon this as an opportunity to identify parallels in the life of Gerry's tiger and those pictured in this album:

M: Where is your favourite tiger? Which one is your tiger, Gerry?

Gerry: (Turning over the pages of the tiger album, Gerry identifies his tiger – this was one of the tigers that his parents had photographed on their visit to the zoo.) There, that's the one!

M: Let me see. This tiger looks happy, doesn't he! I think he's smiling. What do you think Gerry?

Gerry: Yes him does. Him looks happy. (Closely scrutinising the photograph.)

M: What's that? (Pointing to the tiger's mouth.)

Gerry: I dunno.

M: I think that this tiger has been eating beetroot!! I think that these are beetroot stains around his mouth! What do you think Gerry?

Gerry: (Peering at the photograph, and chuckling.) I think him has!

M: Ask your mom and dad what they think.

Parents: (Now huddled around Gerry, pouring over the photograph of the tiger.)

Father: I reckon he has been eating beetroot!

Mother: Didn't use a tissue, did he!

Gerry: (Looking at Michael, and chuckling.) Didn't use a tissue.

M: Didn't he!

Gerry: Let's look for some more. (Placing the tiger album back on Michael's knees.)

M: Okay. (Closely examining the photograph.) What's that! Is that orange peel?

Gerry: Let me see ... (Laughing.)

I met with Gerry and his parents over several more meetings. During this time he went from strength to strength, and his tiger became more and more playful. The family arrived for our fifth meeting with Gerry attempting to hide a large brown paper bag behind his back. After everyone was seated in the interviewing room, Gerry's father indicated that I should leave the room. He followed me to the door and suggested that I come back in a while. I waited for a time, and then loudly announced my return before walking back into the interviewing room:

Father: (Whispering.) Here he comes, here he comes. Quick!

M: (Walking into interviewing room, noticing that Gerry is absent.) Where's Gerry?

Gerry: (A tiger suddenly leaps out from under the chair that Gerry had previously been sitting on.) Roaaaaaaar, Roaaaaaar.

M: (In fright jumps a metre into the air.) Yikes! A tiger! A tiger! Help! Help!

Gerry: Roaaaaaar.

M: (Dives under a chair.) There's a fierce tiger in my room! Help me someone! Help me!

Gerry: It's only me. Look, it's only me.

M: I know, it's a fierce tiger!

Gerry: No, look, it's only me. (Removing his tiger hood, and then peeling off his tiger suit.)

M: Help! Help!

Gerry: It's only me.

M: I know. It's a tiger wearing a little boy suit! Help!

Gerry: (Laughing.)

Parents: (Laughing.)

It did take some time for Gerry to assure me that there was no danger, and to coax me out from under the relative safety of that chair. Although shaken, I mustered my resolve and was able to participate in the rest of the meeting. From what I learned about developments in Gerry's life, it was clear to me that he was now starting to thrive, and was beginning to step into all of the activities he had longed to engage in. Now, twenty years later, I still have a vivid recollection of his pride when, at our last meeting, he walked in to the interviewing room and proudly announced that he had been fishing with his grandfather – we all cried.

Like Richard, Gerry engaged other children in these initiatives. For example, he proudly modelled this tiger suit for his cousins, shared his tiger album with them, and performed a range of tiger feats that were simply breathtaking. His cousins' fascination with these developments in Gerry's life was powerfully reinforcing of Gerry's claims about his tiger identity, and of the initiatives that he was taking in the consumption of food and fluids. And it wasn't long before Gerry's grandmother received several more orders for tiger suits.

Discussion

Externalising conversations also played a significant role in my work with Gerry and his parents. As in my meetings with Richard and Jane, these conversations unfolded according to the same four categories of inquiry of the 'statement of position map, version 1'. First, I invited Gerry and his parents to characterise the problem in terms that were experience-near and particular to Gerry's knowledges of life – this problem became the 'naughty little phobia' ('negotiating an experience-near and particular definition of the problem'). Second, we engaged in an exploration of what this naughty little phobia was up to in their lives and their relationships ('mapping the consequences of the problem's activities'). Third, I inquired about how family members felt about all of this ('evaluating the consequences of the problem's activities). Fourth, Gerry, with the assistance of his parents, helped me to understand why they were all so unhappy about the consequences of the naughty little phobia's activities ('justifying the evaluation'). It was through this inquiry that we all came to a richer understanding of Gerry's longings, and of some of his intentions for his life.

Figure two provides an illustration of the charting of my initial conversation with Gerry and his parents:

Figure 2

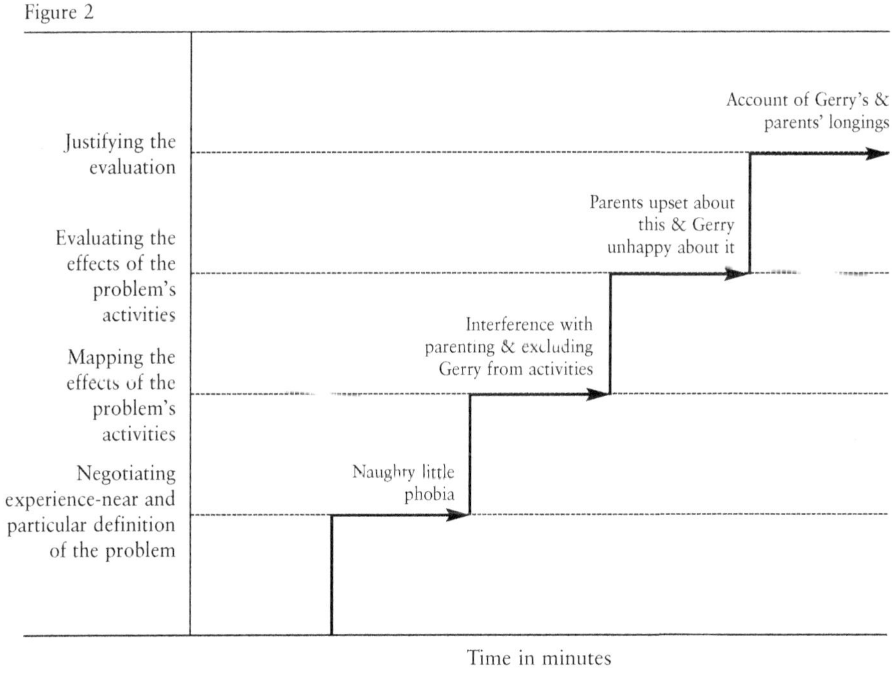

Conclusions about what might be required for Gerry to prevail against the problem were also taken into an externalising conversation. This was shaped by a second version of the statement of position map. The subject of this conversation principally centered on the concept of 'personal strength'. First this strength was characterised – a tiger identity was attributed to it ('negotiating an experience-near and particular definition of the unique outcome/solution/initiative'). Second, we talked about what Gerry's life might look like when this tiger was present, and when he could draw upon tiger strength to do what he wanted ('mapping of the consequences of the unique outcome/solution/initiative'). Third, I enquired about how family members might receive such developments, and I learned that this would be with very considerable enthusiasm ('evaluating the consequences of the unique outcome/solution/initiative'). Fourth, I encouraged family members to provide me with a yet fuller understanding of why they would be so enthusiastic about these developments ('justifying the evaluation').

Figure three provides an illustration of the charting of the initial conversation with Gerry and his parents that was shaped by this second version of the statement of position map. In this conversation the concept of 'strength' was externalised:

Figure 3

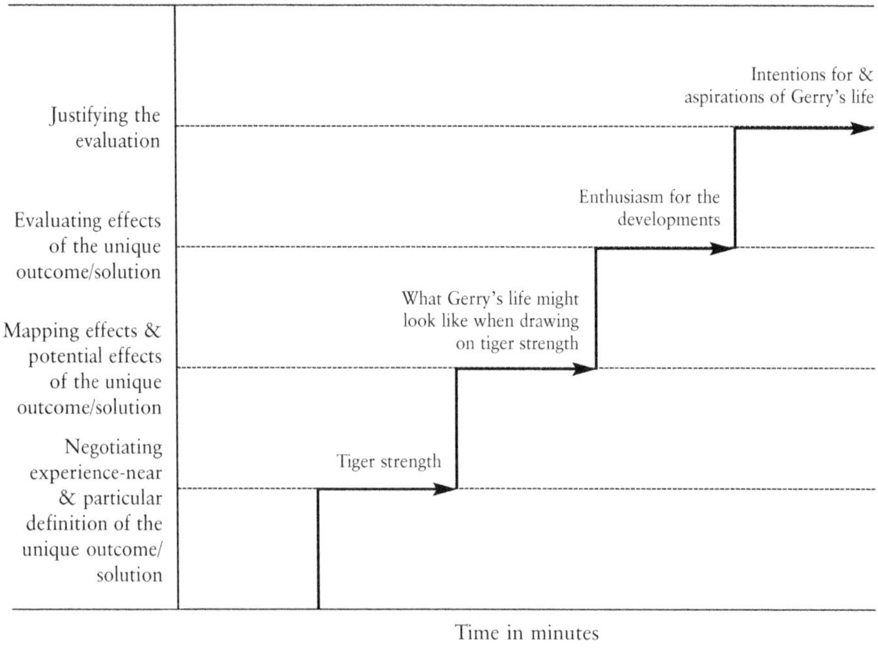

As in my work with Richard and Jane, my conversations with Gerry and his parents did not evolve through these four stages in a strictly linear fashion, but they were progressive. At the outset of the first conversation, the 'eating phobia' which had come to characterise Gerry, defining his existence and his sense of self, was in itself characterised. At the outset of the second conversation, the concept of 'strength' was characterised. At the end of both of these conversations Gerry's identity was being newly described in terms of some of the aspirations and intentions that he had for his life. And, as in my conversations with Richard, this very significantly provided Gerry with a foundation to proceed to address the problem – to proceed in ways that were consistent with this new characterisation of his identity.

Comment

At times it has been assumed that it is only the problems that people present for therapy that are taken into externalising conversations. However, this hasn't been so in the history of my explorations of externalising conversations. Throughout the history of the development of these conversations, I have been just as interested in the part that externalising conversations might play in the revision and redevelopment of what is often defined as people's strengths and resources, and in revisions of people's relationship with whatever it might be that they give value to. Amongst other things, I have explored the possibilities that become available to people as an outcome of entering into externalising conversations in relation to their purposes, hopes, values, beliefs, dreams, and so on. I have found that these conversations open options for people to revise their relationship with what it is that is externalised, and that this provides them with new avenues for addressing their concerns and predicaments.

In my meetings with Gerry and his family there was a double externalisation: first the eating problem was externalised as a naughty little phobia, and then it was tiger strength that became the principle object of our inquiry. The tiger metaphor, which was coined by Gerry in response to my request that he characterise the sort of strength that would be required for him to undertake all of the valued activities that were not available to him, contributed to the externalisation of the phenomenon that is usually conceived as a personal strength. It was through this externalisation that this phenomenon became highly developed and richly known to an extent that would not have been possible had it simply retained the status of an internal quality. And the externalisation of this phenomenon that is usually conceived of as a personal strength provided a foundation for Gerry, with the assistance of his parents, to become more influential in the shaping of his own life.

Millie

Millie, a girl of four years and ten months, was referred to me by child-protection services, with a specific request that I address her difficulties in establishing bowel and bladder regulation. She had persistent soiling and wetting, and this had defied all initiatives undertaken in regard to toilet training. Her foster parents, Sherrie and Ned, had expressed growing concern over this as Millie was about to go to pre-school, and they believed that there was a good chance that she would be rejected by other children on account of her soiling and wetting. Further, they were apprehensive about the possibility that, unless resolved, this problem could contribute to the establishment of a negative reputation that could complicate Millie's relationship with her peers in the school years ahead.

During my initial telephone conversation with the child-protection service worker, she reiterated a request that, in my work with Millie, I specifically focus on the development of bowel and bladder control. She also assured me that the other issues of concern that might become evident in my conversations with Millie and her foster parents were being attended to. These issues of concern were the outcome of the fact that Millie had been through significant trauma in her young life, and exhibited most of the developmental complications that are typically associated with 'failure-to-thrive syndrome'. This included the fact that she was short in stature and was delayed in many of her developmental milestones.

What sort of trauma I asked? The child-protection worker informed me that at the age of two years Millie's biological parents were prosecuted for perpetrating abuse and neglect, and she was removed from their care and placed with foster parents. When Millie was three years and ten months of age, these foster parents were also prosecuted for perpetrating abuse and neglect, and she was placed with a second foster family. In this second foster placement, Millie had 'struck gold'. Under the warm and loving tutelage of these foster parents, Millie's development had accelerated quite dramatically. This was particularly evident in her social skills and in the area of speech development.

There was a further request from the child-protection worker: that I find a way of addressing Millie's problems with bowel and bladder regulation without raising this matter directly with her. 'Oh, is that all. You just simply want me to assist this little girl to achieve this without raising the subject with her', I responded. 'Yeah, that's it', replied the child protection worker. 'Okay, so I've got it. Is there anything else? Like perhaps there is something else that you would like me to do as well that might be a fraction complicated or difficult?' I remarked. This amused the child protection worker, who said that she was making this request on account of the fact that, to date, toilet training initiatives had been traumatising of Millie. In response to these initiatives it was common for Millie to become highly distressed and then to regress. It would then take days before she was again able to pick up the threads of her life. The child protection worker's understanding of this was that Millie's first foster parents had taken to rubbing her face in her own faeces as a method of toilet training her.

It was my sense that the complexities of this situation were such that I would need some assistance in my work with Millie and her foster family. In view of the history of trauma associated with efforts to establish bowel and bladder regulation, and because it would be re-traumatising for Millie to represent herself on this matter, it would be important to have a third party present at our meetings to be her spokesperson. I could interview this spokesperson on matters of soiling and wetting, thus providing a safer context for Millie. The spokesperson could then check back with Millie about the degree of accuracy with which she was being represented.

There was another good reason to engage a third party in this work. Because of the apparently intractable status of Millie's soiling and wetting, I assumed that it would be important for this family to have someone who was readily available to them whom they could consult in their efforts to implement the ideas that might come out of our meetings. Further, I thought that it would be helpful if this person could be available to join the family over these efforts in their home.

In light of these considerations, at my first meeting with this family and the child protection worker I arranged for several of my colleagues to be present. It was my hope that Millie would gravitate towards one of these colleagues, perhaps in the context of play, and strike up a connection with them. It was my intention to then invite this colleague to join me in my work with this family, to represent Millie on the subject of bowel and bladder regulation. At this meeting she did develop such a connection with one of these colleagues, and this colleague was invited to join our meetings as Millie's representative:

M: (Addressing this colleague, who, by the way, happens to be a stuffed toy in the shape of a small bear wearing a pilot's costume, including flying helmet and goggles.) Do you like being with Millie, Pilot?

Millie in role of Pilot responds: Yes.

M: Tell me, do you think that Millie and you will be friends?

Pilot: Yes.

M: He thinks that too! Wow!

Pilot: Yes.

M: Tell me, why would you like Millie for a friend?

Pilot: Because she likes, she likes me.

Michael: Because she likes you! That's a good reason to have Millie for a friend. Will Millie keep you warm?

Pilot: Yes.

M: At night?

Pilot: Yes. And I'll put, and I'll put, she'll put me in my, in my bed.' (Millie briefly dropping out of the role of Pilot, then recapturing this, and then briefly dropping out of it again.)

M: Would you like to cuddle up with Millie in her bed at night?

Pilot: Yes.

M: You would like that! Okay. Tell me, would you like to help Millie get her poos in the toilet?

Pilot: Um, I would teach her how to.

M: You'll teach her how to. Okay. And do you think that you and Millie will be very happy when you teach her how to do that?

Pilot: Yes.

M: How will you teach her how to do that?

Pilot: When Millie comes home from school (pre-school), I'll see ... she will see if ... if I've had a great day.

M: So when Millie gets home from school, she's going to come and ask you whether you had a great day.

Pilot: Yes.

M: What else do you think Millie's going to come and say to you?

Pilot: Mmm. I'm going to help Pilot get poos in the toilet.

M: She is going to tell you that she's going to help you get your poos in the toilet?

Pilot: Mmm. Mmm.

M: And will you help her do that too?

Pilot: Yes.

M: You will? Okay, how would you be able to help Millie get her poos in the toilet?

Pilot: We will go quickly to the toilet.

M: That sounds like a good plan. I think the two of you have a good plan.

Pilot: Yes, yes.

In this meeting it was Pilot's role to be Millie's representative and her consultant. It was through Pilot that Millie was able to express her knowledge about self-regulation and put together a plan – albeit very rudimentary, but in her own words – for addressing the problem of soiling. To the knowledge of the foster parents, this was the first occasion upon which Millie had participated in formulating some ideas for addressing this problem; until this time she had been an unwilling passenger to the ideas formulated by others. Midway through this meeting I consulted all of those present about what they had been drawn to in this conversation between me and Pilot and Millie. In response to this, all present participated in the rich development of the story about Pilot and Millie's connection with each other, and about their plans to address the soiling. Millie listened to this as she drew pictures on a whiteboard, and from time to time interjected with corrections and embellishments.

At the second meeting, three weeks later, I learned that Pilot and Millie had worked well as a team, and that Millie had managed to get 'two poos in the toilet'. About this she was very pleased, and pirouetted to the story of this achievement as it unfolded. Apart from this development, there had been a significant shift in Pilot and Millie's relationship: Millie was now Pilot's consultant, and she was more directly possessing and expressing her knowledge about self-regulation:

Millie: And I got two poos in the toilet!

M: Did you get two in the toilet?

Millie: Yes.

M: Congratulations! Do you shake hands? You got two in the toilet!

Millie: (Nods yes.)

M: Really! And how did you do that?

Millie: I pushed them out.

M: You pushed them out, yeah. And, did Pilot help?

Millie: Yes.

M: How did Pilot help?

Millie: He helped me push them.

M: He helped you push them, did he?

Millie: (Nods yes.) And Pilot pushed the button.

M: What was that?

Millie: When Pilot feels the poo coming out I quickly take him into the toilet.

M: Okay, when Pilot feels the poo coming you quickly take him into the toilet.

Millie: Yes, and he does a poo.

M: And he does a poo.

Millie: In the toilet.

M: Really, wow! So Pilot lets you know. Pilot tells you when it's a good time.

Millie: Yes.

M: Does he? That's great, yeah! And were you ...

Sherri (Millie's foster mother): And she's sitting longer.

M: Sorry?

Sherri: I said she's just sitting longer ...

Millie: I try to, I sit for a long time on the toilet.

M: Oh, okay, so there's two things, you sit longer as well do you?

Sherri: Yes she does. And I don't have to remind her quite so often, sometimes she tells me she's going to sit and try.

Millie: Yep.

M: So two things. You got poos in the toilet twice – can I write this down here?

Millie: Yes.

M: I'll just put here: 'Millie put poos in the toilet two times', yeah. (Michael begins to recite as he writes, and Millie quickly commandeers this, rendering Michael the scribe.)

Sherri: You tell Michael ... what else did you want to say? You were sitting, were you going to tell Michael that? You sit a little bit better now it's not so hard to sit still?

Millie: Yeah, I sit a little better now. It isn't hard to sit still.

M: Millie sits better now, and ... (Again, Michael begins to recite as he writes, and again Millie quickly commandeers this.)

Millie: ... and it isn't hard to sit still, no it's not.

M: And you said that Pilot helped. Can I write down what Pilot said again? What you told me about Pilot? You said Pilot tells you when the poo's coming, yeah.

Millie: And I tell Pilot when he, and then I take Pilot to the toilet quickly and he does a poo in the toilet.

M: Okay. And I take Pilot, I take Pilot quickly ... (Michael again writing, and almost instantaneously back in the position as scribe to Millie's voice on this.)

Millie: ... to the toilet, and he does poos in the toilet.

M: Wow, that's what I've written there. See, I've put here: Millie put poos in the toilet two times. And Millie sits better now, it isn't hard to sit still. And then Pilot tells Millie when poo is coming and Millie takes him quickly to the toilet and he does poos in the toilet! (At this point Millie is intently pouring over the written word, which is clearly profoundly significant to her, even though she does not read or write.)

Millie: Yes.

M: And were you happy. Happy when you got poos in the toilet? Or were you sad when you got poos in the toilet? Or ...

Millie: Happy ...

M: Who else was happy? Anybody else happy?

Millie: Barry was. (Barry is Millie's elder foster brother.)

M: Barry was happy?

Sherri: He had to come and have a look didn't he! (Laugh.)

Millie: And I done big poos in the toilet.

M: You did big poos in the toilet. Okay. And how did you know? Did you hear a plop, or what?

Sherri: What did you tell me Millie ... what did you tell me? I said: 'How did you know there was a poo there?' What did you tell me? Do you remember what you told me?

Millie: Oh, yeah.

Sherri: What did you say? What could you feel? Do you remember what you told me?

Millie: A poo coming.

M: Yeah, you felt a poo coming.

Sherri: And you felt it coming out you told me, didn't you. So you knew there was something there, you had to have a look, yeah ... so she's never actually said that before.

M: So, you felt a poo coming out ...

Millie: Yeah. I felt a poo coming.

M: Did you? Wow. And that's something that you saw as particularly important?

Sherri: Mmm, because she's never ever said this. She just sort of keeps peeping there not knowing if there's anything there or not, but she said she knew because she could feel it coming out.

M: Okay. So before she had to keep peeping, and now she can actually tell when it's coming?

Sherri: Mmm, they're only tiny ones. And she goes quickly now when it's very fresh in her pants, so obviously she's not quite finished so she can do a little bit more in there, so I guess that's stage one.

By the third meeting, Millie had become Pilot's teacher, even more directly possessing and expressing her knowledge in relation to the establishment of self-regulation. She had also recruited a third member onto the team – a new doll – and the three of them had been going off to the toilet room to do their thing together while sitting on each other's lap. The logistics of this sounded rather hazardous, but it appeared to be working out quite well!

Several meetings into our work together, Millie showed up with a medallion around her neck. This was a medallion that her foster brother had won in a bicycle competition some years earlier. At the time of this meeting the Australian Olympic Games were in full swing, and I correctly assumed that Millie had been watching the medal ceremonies on television. I openly wondered whether Millie deserved a progress medal for what she had so far achieved, and all present concurred. I offered to organise this, and interviewed Millie about what she would like to have inscribed on the medal. I left these words with the manager of a trophy store, along with instructions to produce a medal that was a replica of those presented at the Australian Olympic Games. The plan was to award this medal to Millie at 'a presentation evening', in the manner in which certain sports people are awarded medals by their clubs at the end of each season.

The 'presentation evening' duly took place late on a Thursday afternoon, and was attended by invited family and friends. In the ceremonial phase of this meeting, Millie stood on a dias that I'd assembled, one that was replete with giant blue and gold ribbons, while those present had the opportunity to speak about their understandings of Millie's achievement. Millie was clearly in 'heaven' at this time, and on account of her excitement I was concerned that she might fall from the dias. The shiny medal was then awarded to her, and we all sang the Australian National Anthem, as Millie had become familiar with this from watching the medal presentations to Australian swimmers. As the Australian National Anthem is not generally well-known, I'd handed around copies of this and had also played an audio-recording of it so that everyone would know the words and could sing to the tune. Even with these preparations, two of the participants of this event got into a debate about whether this really was the national anthem, and this was only resolved when I said that it really didn't matter and that we could just sing it anyway.

This ceremonial phase of the presentation evening was followed by a celebratory phase in which we all consumed the sweets, cakes and liquid refreshments that had been ordered by Millie (I recall feeling a little nauseous at the end of this event). The presentation evening contributed to an acceleration of Millie's progress, and before long she had successfully achieved the 'accident free' regulation of her bowel and bladder.

A few months after follow-up, Millie's foster mother, Sherrie, called to say that she was again concerned about Millie. This concern was not about regress – Millie had remained incident free in regard to bowel and bladder regulation. Rather, Millie, now six years of age, had recently begun to talk about 'the mean things' that had been done to her in her first foster home. As she was nearly four years of age before being removed from this context, it could be expected that she would have had clear episodic memories of some of her experiences of trauma.

This development had caused Sherrie and Ned, Millie's foster father, much consternation. On the one hand, these parents were concerned that to encourage conversations about this trauma might be very unsettling for a little girl whose life was only now becoming settled – in fact she was just about to sleep over at a friend's house, and would be soon going away on a brief school camp (a two-day and one night visit to a nature reserve). On the other hand, these parents understood that it could be important for Millie to give expression to her experiences of trauma, and that this should be welcomed, and not silenced or discouraged.

Sherrie hoped that I might be able to assist in resolving this dilemma by telling her how to approach it. I informed her that it was my understanding that trauma had different effects on different children, and, as well, that a response to an expression of trauma that is appropriate for one child might not be appropriate for another. I suggested that the family return for a further meeting so that we might have an opportunity to figure out what would work for Millie. Before long I was meeting with Sherrie and Ned while Millie was being cared for by our reception person. At the outset of this meeting I said that I had a proposal for how we might find out what would work best for Millie at those times when she was giving expression to the trauma she'd been through. Ned, however, was very insistent that I would know how to advise them in regard to this dilemma:

Ned: Surely you'd know what to do about this Michael. I know you see lots of kids who've had hard times, and you must have come across this situation many times before. Surely you'd know what to do.

M: It's my experience that every situation is different, and what works for one child doesn't necessarily work for another.

Ned: But surely Michael this isn't a different child. Surely you know Millie better than most know her, so surely, surely you of all people, surely you would know what to suggest.

M: Yeah, I do know Millie. But I really don't know what is going to work best for her in this situation that's about healing responses. I think that we are going to have to do something that is tailor-made. And I've got an idea about how we might get onto that.

Ned: Okay, let's get going. Let's have it then.

I then shared my proposal for how we might proceed. Sherrie and Ned approved of this, and Millie soon joined us. I introduced Millie to another two of my colleagues, Toby and Julie, both stuffed toys. I then told her a story about Toby and Julie that closely paralleled her own story:

M: Millie, I wanted you to meet Julie and Toby, who have been with me for about as long as you have been with your new mum and dad. When Julie and Toby first came to live with me they were really scared. They didn't feel very good, and they didn't know if they could trust me.

Millie: Oh.

M: But after a while they began to feel safe with me. They began to feel much better, and then they began to get happier.

Millie: Oh.

M: Now Toby and Julie are feeling so safe and so good that they are both going to sleep over with friends next week. This will be their very first time.

Millie: Like me! That's like me!

M: And soon they are going to go away on a school camp.

Millie: Just like me!

M: But I have been worried about them.

Millie: Why?

M: Because I am about to go away with my work for about four weeks, and it just isn't a good time for me to go. Just when Julie and Toby are sleeping over for the first time, and just when they are going on their first school camp, they really need me to be there for them. It's not a good time for me to go, is it?

Millie: (Pauses, looking at me in a disapproving way – in fact so disapproving that I have a sense that she is entertaining the idea of calling the child protection service about my negligence!) No, it isn't. (Now shaking her head.)

M: Anyway, I have found a lovely family for one of them to stay with, where I know they will be alright while I am away. Would you be happy to look after the other one?

Millie: (Immediately seizing Toby, and holding him to her chest.) I'll take Toby. I'll take Toby. I'll look after him.

M: Phew! Thank you Millie. Thank you so much. Now I won't worry, because I know that Toby will be in safe hands while I am away.

Millie: I'll look after you Toby.

M: Millie, I have to tell you something. Toby has just started to talk about some of the mean things that were done to him before he came to live with me.

Millie: Ohhh. (Now stroking Toby, and holding him more tightly to her chest.)

M: And he might want to talk to you about some of these mean things while I'm away. Would that be alright?

Millie: Yeah, that would be alright.

M: Toby might feel a bit sad when he talks about these mean things.

Millie: That's alright.

M: What will you do if he does feel sad.

Millie: Pick him up and cuddle him. Make sure that he isn't by himself at night. And give him special treats.

M: (Briefly looking in the direction of the foster parents, hoping they are catching this, and that they will take their cue from this in responding to Millie when she talks about the trauma she experienced in her first foster home.)

Sherri: (Looks relieved and winks, signalling to me that she now has an answer to this dilemma about how to respond on such occasions.)

M: (Looking to Ned for a sign that this dilemma is also resolved for him.)

Ned: Michael, why are you staring at me?

M: (Turning away from Ned briefly, hoping that more time for reflection might assist him to 'get it', then turning back to him.)

Ned: (This time he gives me a highly theatrical and overdone wink, and then laughs uproariously – I always appreciated Ned's fondness for his own humour.)

M: (Thinking that it is now my turn.) What's wrong with your right eye Ned?

Ned: Nothing. Nothing.

Millie: Yes there is Dad, I saw it too. What's wrong with your eye Dad?

M: Millie, I'm a bit worried about your dad. He has this strange tick thing in his eye, and he calls me Shirley all the time.(Ned had the habit of prefacing many of his questions to me with the words: 'Surely Michael ...'. For an example of this, see previous except of transcript.)

Millie, Sherri, Ned, and M: (All laughing.)

Six weeks later, following my return to Adelaide, I again met with Millie and her foster parents. Millie's sleep-over had been successful, and she was just back from her school camp, which had also gone well. Both Toby and Pilot had accompanied her on these adventures. I asked about how everything had been for Toby in my absence, and about how things had worked out between him and Millie. I also asked if Toby had been talking to her about some of the mean things that had been done to him before he came to live with me. She affirmed that this was the case:

M: And you've been looking after Toby?

Millie: Yep.

M: And you were going to talk to Toby, because when he was little, before he came to live with me, some people were very mean to him like they were mean to you. Remember?

Millie: Yeah.

M: And I was going to be away for a little bit and I was worried about Toby. He needed someone to look after him, and you said that you'd look after him. And have you been talking to him?

Millie: Yep.

M: What have you been telling Toby?

Millie: Oh, that, that's alright.

M: You have been telling him 'that's alright'.

Millie: Yeah. And he gets scared in the night sometimes.

M: He gets scared in the night sometimes?

Millie: That's when I pick him up and hug him.

M: You pick him up and hug him. So he feels nice and safe when he's with you?

Millie: Yep.

M: And you tell him everything will be alright?

Millie: Yep.

M: Did he say anything about some of the mean things that were done to him.

Millie: Oh, he said he didn't like it.

M: What else did he say?

Millie: Um, he said, he said he loves me.

M: He loves you – he said he loves you, did he?

Millie: He wants to stay at my house.

Sherri: (Laughs.) But he's Dr Michael's bear, so should he stay at our house, or has he got a house of his own?

Ned: All his friends and little brothers and sisters here will miss him.

Millie: Has he got a house?

M: He does have a house, but I was wondering if you wouldn't mind looking after him a little bit longer, because I am going away again, and I think he will be lonely if he doesn't stay with you.

Millie: Don't let him stay with those mean people again.

M: No, he should never stay with those mean people again, should he?

Over the next thirty minutes the account of Millie's healing responses were more fully drawn out. It turned out that she was a veritable fount of ideas when it came to assisting Toby in regard to the traumas he'd suffered. I also learned that Millie had come to Sherrie and Ned with stories of the mean things that Toby had been subject to. At these times they responded in ways consistent with what they knew of Millie's healing knowledges – for example, they would listen carefully, then immediately pick her up, cuddle her, ensure that she wasn't alone at night, and give her special treats.

Discussion

Millie's sense of herself and of life had been considerably defined by her experience of trauma. Although the concerted efforts of her second foster parents and the child protection agency had made very significant inroads on this before Millie met Pilot, it was clear that this experience of trauma held sway in circumstances in which toilet training was at issue. In these circumstances, Millie was prone to re-experiencing this trauma, and this had the effect of recuperating a passive-recipient identity status, and strong sense of incompetence – which was all that it was possible for her to know about herself under these circumstances.

Pilot's participation provided Millie with the opportunity to reposition herself in conversations about bowel and bladder regulation. In this repositioning, Millie was able to distance from the immediacy of her experience of trauma and to experience a degree of separation from this passive-recipient identity status. This distancing from the known and familiar, from this customary sense of identity associated with trauma, opened the possibility for Millie to define and give expression to her knowledge of self-regulation. From our first meeting, re-positioned as Pilot, she derived a course of action that she believed would contribute to success with toilet training. Admittedly, in the first place, this was founded upon a very rudimentary plan, but this marked the first occasion upon which Millie had a voice in regard to this issue.

In the second meeting Millie was positioned as Pilot's consultant, thus more directly embracing of her knowledge of self-regulation. However, she was still at a distance from the passive recipient identity status, and from the immediacy of her experience of trauma in regard to toilet training, as this was now projected onto Pilot. It was from this distance that Millie then more fully embraced and developed her knowledge of self-regulation, becoming, by our third meeting, Pilot's teacher, as the status of this knowledge was increasingly elevated within the context of our conversations.

These developments were further supported through soliciting responses from Millie's foster parents, foster brother, and from the child-protection worker. I invited them to reflect on what they perceived to be the actual and potential consequences of these developments in Millie's life, on what these developments reflected about Millie's friendship skills, and about what these suggested about what she wanted for her life; about what these developments might say about her purposes, her plans, and her hopes. Before long, Millie was reproducing many of these concepts about life in her conversations with Pilot and her foster parents.

When Sherrie called about her dilemma over how she might respond to Millie's stories about the trauma that she was subject to in her first foster home, my thoughts went to how to structure a context that would foreground Millie's knowledge about healing responses, and contribute to the further development of these. I understood that the foster parents would have some familiarity with a knowledge about healing responses that would be relevant to Millie, for this would have been significantly developed in the context of their relationship with her, and in the context of their contribution to her learnings about life.

However, I perceived an opportunity to bring to focus a knowledge of healing responses that might be particularly relevant to Millie, and in a way that might assist her to distance from the immediacy of her experience of trauma.

The introduction of Toby and Julie set the scene for this. The parallels drawn between their lives and Millie's life established a strong sense of identification with them. In forewarning Millie that Toby might tell her about the mean things that he'd been subject to, conditions were established for her to step back from the immediacy of her experiences of trauma, and to instead represent Toby to her foster parents on these experiences. From this more distant position, Millie was able to enact and further develop her knowledge of healing responses. These were played out in her interaction with Toby, and reproduced by the foster parents in their responses to the stories Millie began to bring to them. Apart from rendering this knowledge of responses more available to Millie, Toby's participation contributed to a context of safety for Millie – she could now give expression to her experiences of trauma without being defined by these experiences.

Comment

In the therapeutic conversations with Richard and Jane, it was the problem that was externalised. This provided an opportunity for Richard to distance from the ways that he had been defined by the problem; from a principal known and familiar sense of identity associated with the experience of fears. In the therapeutic conversations with Gerry and his parents, it was both the problem and the conception of strength that was externalised. This provided an opportunity for Gerry to also distance from a principal known and familiar sense of his identity, and for him and his parents to more richly know and develop this conception of personal strength. In the therapeutic conversations with Millie and her foster parents, it was incompetence, traumatic experience and knowledges of self-regulation that were externalised. Subsequently, these knowledges of self-regulation were more directly embraced by Millie, and further developed.

Scaffolding the zone of proximal development: a second interpretation of narrative practice.

In the illustrations given in this chapter, externalising practices assisted Richard, Gerry, and Millie, and the members of their families, to distance from the principal known and familiar accounts of their lives, and from experiences of life associated with these accounts, and to move towards what it was possible for these children to know about their lives, and for others to know about the lives of these children. This was an incremental and progressive distancing from this known and familiar that is not synonymous with a splitting off from one's life. Rather, it was an incremental and progressive distancing that provided a foundation for these children to play a more significant part in influencing the course of their own development and, in so doing, to more fully inhabit their own lives.

There is always some distance between the known and the familiar on the one hand, and what it is possible for people to know and to do on the other. This is a gap that must be traversed in order for people to have more to say about the shape of their lives and their relationships. It is rarely possible for people to traverse this gap without the appropriate scaffolding. This is the sort of scaffolding that is the outcome of social collaboration; that is founded upon the supportive participation of others. In my meetings with Richard, Gerry and Millie, I contributed significantly to this scaffolding in various ways, but principally through the introduction of various categories of inquiry associated with externalising practices. I also recruited the participation of Richard, Gerry and Millie's family members, other relatives, friends, and a child-protection worker, in this scaffolding. Richard and Gerry, on their own initiatives, recruited the participation of peers and cousins.

In traversing this gap between the known and the familiar and what it is possible to know and to do, Richard, Gerry and Millie all experienced a newfound sense of personal agency. By 'personal agency' I am referring to that sense of being able to regulate one's own life; to intervene in one's life to effect its course according to one's intentions, and to do this in ways that are shaped by one's knowledges of life and skills of living. It is this sense of personal agency that makes it possible for people to engage in what is usually regarded to be 'responsible' action in relation to the predicaments and problems of their lives. According to this understanding, responsible action is not the outcome of chance, of the 'liberation' of 'human nature', or of any developmental imperative. Nor is it simply a 'construct'. Rather, 'responsibility' is founded upon the development of a sense of personal agency which is in turn the outcome of a special sort of social collaboration.

These terms – 'distancing', 'scaffolding', 'social collaboration', 'personal agency' – invoke the work of the Russian psychologist, Lev Vygotsky (1986), a developmental theorist who had special interest in early-childhood learning. Although the development of my work with families with children was not originally informed by Vygotsky's thought, in recent years I have been drawn to many of his ideas. This is principally because I find that my therapeutic explorations are confirming of Vygotsky's conclusions about learning and development. I also find that his ideas contribute to new understandings of processes of therapeutic change, lend clarity to what is significant in the conversations of narrative therapy, and reinforce various narrative practices. And, as well, I am finding that his ideas are contributing to the further development of some of my narrative practices. On account of this, I have decided to briefly review some of Vygotsky's ideas in the last section of this chapter.

The zone of proximal development

Vygotsky was primarily interested in explorations of early childhood development. In these explorations he determined that, in a great majority of cases, development is founded upon learning. This was a challenge to much of the prevailing developmental theory of his time that asserted that development preceded learning and that, on this basis, learning was the outcome of the unfolding of some genetic/neurological imperative.

Vygotsky also emphasised that learning was an achievement not of independent effort, but of social collaboration. In this social collaboration, he observed that adult caretakers and more sophisticated peers structure children's learning in ways that make it possible for them to move from what is known and familiar to them, and from routine achievements, to what it is possible for them to know and to achieve. This he described as a movement across a zone of learning that he termed the 'zone of proximal development'. This is a zone that is comprised of the distance between what the child can know and achieve independently and what it is possible for the child to know and to achieve in collaboration with others.

Traversing this zone requires that the child distance from the immediacy of their experience. It is a significant task. According to Vygotsky, this is not a task that children can achieve unless it is broken down into manageable portions. It is the part that caretakers and more sophisticated peers play in this that contributes to the 'scaffolding' of this zone of proximal development. This scaffolding encourages the child to 'stretch' his/her mind and to 'exercise' his/her imagination in the achievement of these learning tasks, but not in ways that require impossible or improbable leaps that would contribute to exhaustion and a sense of failure on behalf of the child.

Vygotsky proposed that it was through this progressive and incremental distancing from the already known and familiar, and from the immediacy of one's experience, that it becomes possible for children to develop 'chains of association' that establish bonds and relations between what would otherwise simply remain undifferentiated objects and events of their worlds. He referred to this as the development of 'complex thinking', and he demonstrated how the development of this complex thinking provides the basis for the development of 'concepts' about life and identity.

It is this conceptual development that supplies the foundation for people to regulate their lives: to influence their own actions in purposeful ways; to intervene in their own lives to shape the course of events; and to problem-solve. According to this understanding, those actions that are considered to be responsible and autonomous have their foundation in social collaboration, without which this responsible and autonomous action would not be possible. The achievement of this self-regulation is synonymous with what I have referred to as the development of 'personal agency'.

I will here summarise some of Vygotsky's principal ideas about the zone of proximal development, and about learning. In seeking to reveal the genesis of learning, Vygotsky's research brought him to the following conclusions:

a) Learning is the outcome of social collaboration, not of independent effort, or of the unfolding of any 'hard-wired' bio-genetic process. In this social collaboration, skilled caretakers and sophisticated peers provide supported learning tasks that are within the reach of the child, but that require the investment of significant effort on behalf of the child.

b) It is through these learning tasks that children have the opportunity to distance from the immediacy of their experience of the world. This is a movement towards what they might know and do in collaboration with others.

c) This is a movement across a zone of learning that he called the 'zone of proximal development'. This is a zone that is formed by the distance between what the child can know and achieve independently and what it is possible for the child to know and to achieve in collaboration with others. To quote Vygotsky, the zone of proximal development is: *the distance between the actual developmental level as determined by independent problem solving and the level of potential development as determined through problem solving under adult guidance or in collaboration with more capable peers ...* (1986, p.86)

d) In this movement across this zone, there is a shift from gathering the objects and events of the world into 'heaps', from the uniting of diverse objects and events in groups under a common family name, to gathering the objects and events of the world into chains of association, or into complexes, that establish bonds and relations between these objects and events.

e) There are several levels in the development of these chains of association or formation of complexes, from the preliminary unification of objects and events on the basis of maximum similarity to the grouping of objects and events on the basis of a single attribute (for example, only round objects or flat objects).

f) This development of complex thinking provides a foundation for the development of 'concepts'. To quote Vygotsky, the development of a concept: *presupposes more than unification. To form such a concept it is also necessary to abstract, to single out elements, and to view the abstracted elements apart from the totality of the concrete experience in which they are embedded.* (1986, p.135)

g) This conceptual development provides a foundation for the child to intervene in shaping their own actions and in the constitution of their own lives. According to Vygotsky, on account of this development, the child is now able to operate with these concepts at will and as a task demands, and with a consciousness of these operations, understanding them to be processes of a certain kind. In his terms, it is this development that leads to 'self-mastery' in intellectual functions: for example, he asserts that this concept development is the foundation of *deliberate attention, logical memory, abstraction, the ability to compare and to differentiate.* In terms that I have employed in this chapter, this development of conceptual thought can be considered the foundation of 'personal agency'. It is through the development of conceptual thought that children begin to inhabit their own lives.

h) Language and word-meaning evolution is crucial to this conceptual development – the pathway to concept formation is the development of word-meanings. To quote Vygotsky again: *When a new word has been learned by the child, its development is barely starting; as the child's intellect develops, it is replaced by generalizations of a higher and higher type – a process that leads in the end to the formation of true concepts … Real concepts are impossible without words, and thinking in concepts does not exist beyond verbal thinking. That is why the central movement in concept formation, and its generative cause, is a specific use of words as functional tools.* (1986, p.107)

The zone of proximal development and therapeutic practice

The focus of Vygotsky's research was early childhood development, and it was his intention to identify those early childhood educational practices that were most favourable to child development. However, his conclusions are relevant to considerations of learning and development at all 'stages and ages'. And I have also found these conclusions to be relevant to the further understanding of effective therapeutic practices, and to the further development of these therapeutic practices.

People consult therapists when they are having difficulty in proceeding with their lives. In these circumstances, in their efforts to address their predicaments and concerns, it is usually the case that people are reproducing the known and the familiar; they are engaging in actions that are in keeping with familiar conclusions about their lives and relationships, and with customary knowledges about life. The gap between this known and familiar and what it might be possible for people to know and do can be considered a 'zone of proximal development'.

This zone cannot be traversed without the sort of conversational partnership that would provide the necessary scaffolding to achieve this; that is, the sort of scaffolding that would provide the opportunity for people to proceed across this zone in manageable steps. In the context of therapeutic practice, the therapist contributes significantly to the scaffolding of the proximal zone of development, and also recruits the participation of others in this. This scaffolding makes it possible for people who are consulting therapists to incrementally and progressively distance from the known and familiar towards what it might be possible for them to know and to do.

Influenced by the ideas of Vygotsky, I have developed a 'scaffolding conversations' map that is structured by five categories of inquiry. This map can be utilised to provide a guide to the development of therapeutic conversations that facilitate incremental and progressive movements across the proximal zone of learning. The categories of inquiry of this map establish specific learning tasks, which I define as:

a) Low-level distancing tasks; that is, tasks that encourage people to characterise specific objects and events of their worlds,

b) Medium-level distancing tasks; that is, tasks that encourage people to bring into relationship specific objects and events of their world in the development of chains of association, or 'complexes', that establish bonds and relations between these objects and events.

c) Medium high-level distancing tasks; that is, tasks that encourage people to reflect on these chains of association and to draw, from these, realisations and learnings about specific phenomena.

d) High-level distancing tasks; that is, tasks that encourage people to abstract these realisations and learnings from their concrete and specific circumstances in order to form concepts about life and identity.

e) Very high-level distancing tasks; that is, tasks that encourage the formulation of predictions about the outcome of specific actions founded upon this concept development, and tasks that encourage the planning for and initiation of such actions.

Statement of position map, version 1 revisited

At the beginning of my conversations with Richard and Jane, I supported the characterisation of Richard's fears (which were painted and named, which became known in their operations and activities, and which were identified in terms of their agenda for his life). In the 'statement of position map, vesion 1', this initiative was defined as 'developing an experience-near and particular definition of the problem'. In the scaffolding conversations map this characterisation of the problem would be typified as a 'low-level distancing task'. For Gerry and his parents, the initial low-level distancing tasks encouraged them to characterise the problem, which became 'the naughty little phobia'.

In the second phase of my conversation with Richard and Jane, I encouraged them to bring the problem into relationship with its consequences (which included sleeplessness, fearfulness, isolation from peers, and exclusion from education). In the 'statement of position map 1' this was defined as 'mapping the effects/influence of the problem'. In the scaffolding conversations map this would be typified as a 'medium-level distancing task'. For Gerry and his parents, this medium-level distancing task encouraged them to link the activities of the 'naughty little phobia' to specific consequences in their lives (which included exclusion of Gerry from activities like climbing trees, playing with his peers, riding a bike, and going fishing with his grandfather, and which constantly demanded his parents' attention and interfered in their parenting of him).

In the third phase of my conversations with Richard and Jane, I supported them in reflecting on the operations and activities of the fears, and the consequences of these operations and activities. As an outcome of this, both spoke of their experience of these operations and activities, and of their consequences and, as well, gave voice to certain realisations (which included various expressions of indignation and displeasure, and the realisation that the fears needed a good education). In the statement of position map, version 1, this was defined as 'evaluating the effects of the problem's activities and operations'. In the 'scaffolding conversations map' this would be typified as a 'medium-high level distancing task'. For Gerry and his parents, it was in the context of this medium-high level distancing task that they gave voice to their frustrations and to their disapproval of the havoc that the naughty little phobia was creating.

In the fourth phase of my conversations with Richard and Jane, I supported them in reflecting on these experiences and realisations, and in giving voice to conclusions about what this said about what they intended for their lives and about what they give value to (which included a range of hopes and fear-free plans for Richard's future). In terms of the statement of position map, version 1., this was referred to as 'justifying the evaluation'. In the scaffolding conversations map, this would be typified as a 'high-level distancing task', with these conclusions representing concepts about life and identity. For Gerry and his family it was in the context of this high-level distancing task that he renewed his goal of going fishing with his grandfather.

In the fifth phase of my conversations with Richard and Jane, I supported them in speculating about what steps might be taken to address the predicament at hand, steps that would be in harmony with their conclusions about what they intended for their lives, and with what they accorded value. In the scaffolding conversations map this would be typified as a very high-level distancing task. For Gerry, one high-level distancing task had him making plans to stand aside to allow the tiger to feed.

Figure four provides an illustration of the charting of my consultation with Richard and Jane according to the scaffolding conversations map:

Figure 4

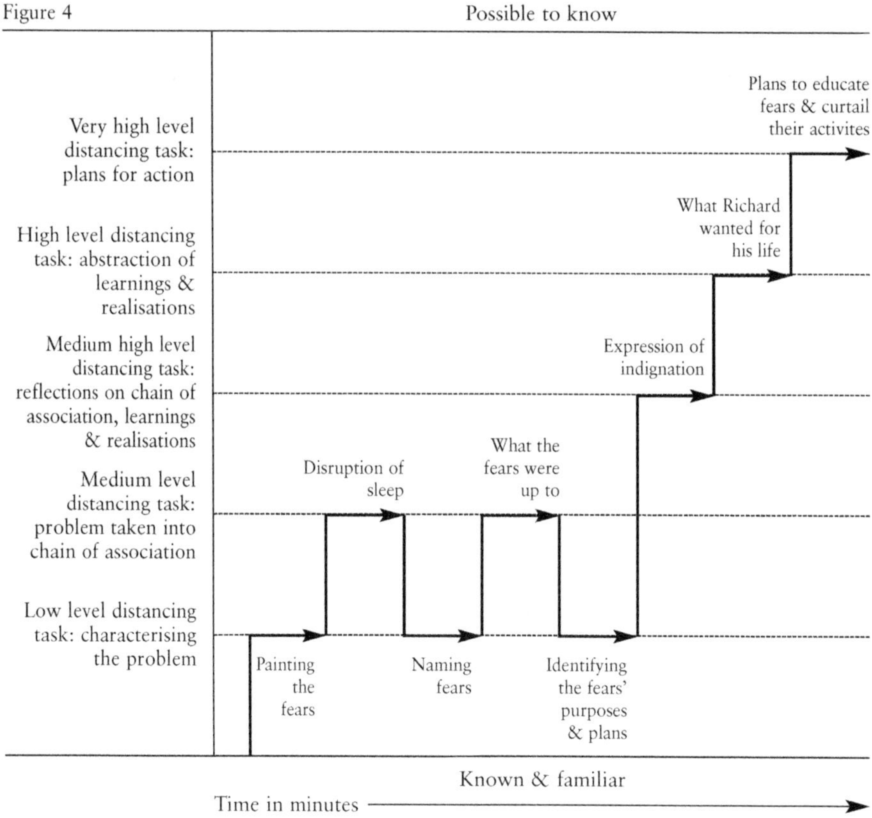

Figure five provides an illustration of the charting of my consultation with Gerry and his parents according to the scaffolding conversations map:

Figure 5

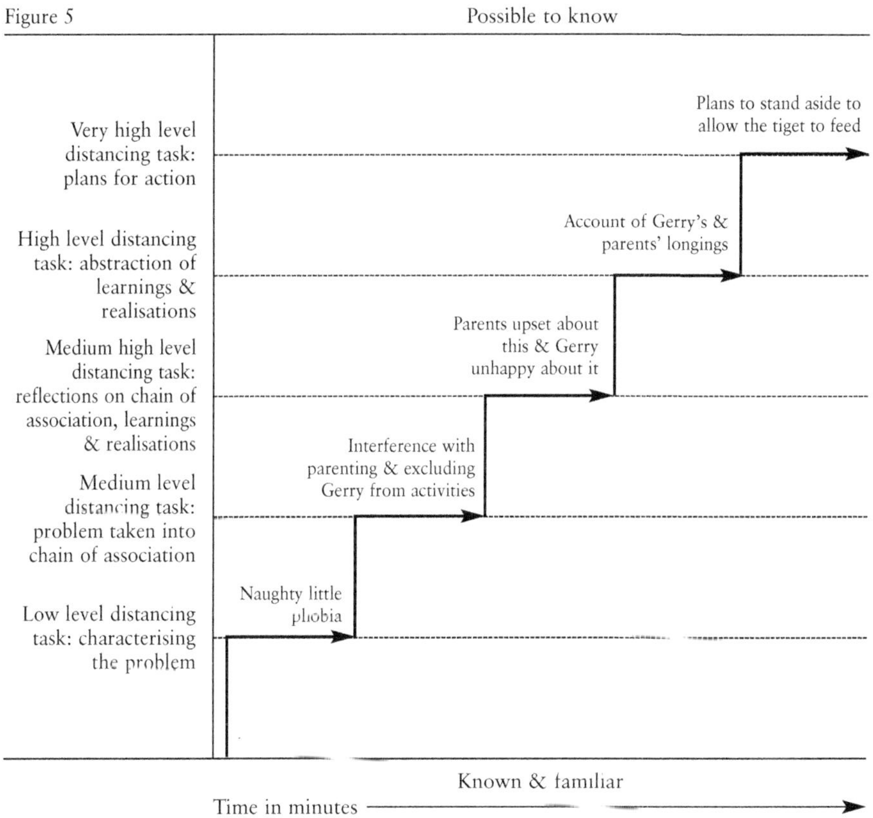

Statement of position map, version 2 revisited

When Gerry gave voice to the significant part that strength could play in reclaiming his life from the 'naughty little phobia', I encouraged and supported the characterisation of this strength (it became 'tiger strength'). In the statement of position map, version 2, this was defined as 'negotiating an experience-near and particular definition of the unique outcome/initiative'. In the scaffolding conversations map, this would be typified as a 'low-level distancing task'.

I then encouraged Gerry and his parents to draw out the consequences/potential consequences of the tiger's activities in his life (which included playing with friends, riding a bike, and climbing trees). In the statement of position map, verson 2, this was defined as 'mapping the effects or potential effects of the unique outcome/initiative'. In the scaffolding conversations map it would be typified as a 'medium-level distancing task'.

Next, Gerry and his parents were encouraged to give voice to their experiences of these developments/potential developments (which included unreserved enthusiasm), and to describe some of the realisations associated with this. In terms of the statement of position map, version 2, this was defined as 'evaluating the effects of the unique outcome/initiative'. In the scaffolding conversations map it would be typified as a 'medium-high level distancing task'.

I then supported Gerry and his parents in reflecting on these experiences and realisations to determine what this said about what he intended for his life, and about what he gave value to (which included a much richer description of all of those plans for the future that the 'naughty little phobia' had frustrated). In terms of the statement of position map, version 2, this was defined as 'justifying the evaluation'. In the scaffolding conversations map it would be typified as a 'high-level distancing task'.

Lastly, I encouraged Gerry and his parents to speculate about steps that might be possible for him that would be in harmony with what we'd all been learning about in terms of what he intended for his own life. In the scaffolding conversations map this would be typified as a 'very high-level distancing task'.

Figure 6

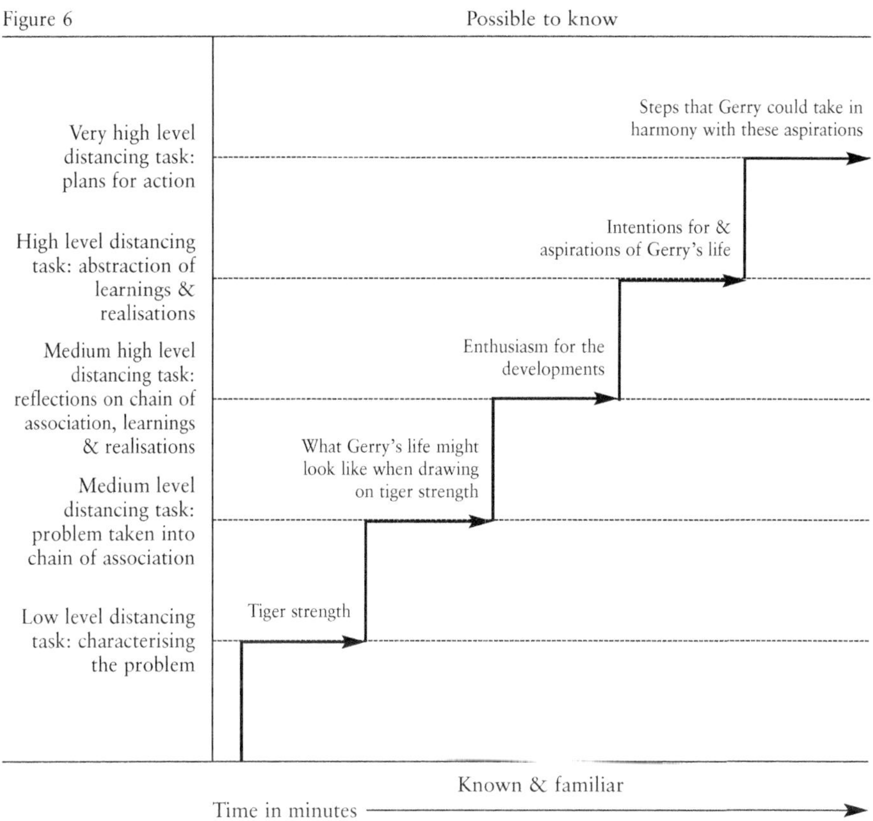

Repositioning and scaffolding the zone of proximal development

At this juncture, I will reiterate some of my reflections on my meetings with Millie and her family, with further emphasis on the part that repositioning played in the scaffolding of her zone of proximal development.

The categories of inquiry of the externalising conversations maps were also very present in my work with Millie and her foster parents. However, on account of the potential for Millie to be re-traumatised in any direct consultation about the problems of soiling and wetting, in the first place I went to special lengths to establish an opportunity for her to speak from a position that wasn't defined by this problem and by the trauma of her history. In this development, she re-positioned herself as Pilot, and as a consultant to Millie. As a consultant to Millie, some of her knowledges about life and skills in self-regulation were further developed, and became available to her in her efforts to address the problem that was now characterised as 'poos', which came to occupy a third position. As Pilot, this little girl was distanced from the experience of trauma associated with toilet training, from negative conclusions about Millie's identity (that she was bad, incompetent, and a failure), and from 'poos'.

As our work progressed, these three positions were maintained, but there was a shift in that this little girl stepped out of the Pilot position and re-occupied the Millie position, becoming Pilot's teacher, and Poos' educator. This shift occurred as she became more knowledged about the problem and the solution, and as this contributed to possibilities for the redevelopment of Millie's identity.

Later, in response to the foster parents' concerns that revisiting memories of trauma could be profoundly destabilising of Millie, I again established an opportunity for her to speak from a position that wasn't defined by the trauma of her history. This was also an opportunity for Millie to distance from the immediacy of her experience. However, on this occasion she was able to take her identity with her. As Millie, she was able to give representation to Toby's experience of trauma without being defined by this, and was free to further develop healing knowledges and to respond with these. In representing these experiences of trauma and her healing knowledges in this way, she provided her foster parents with options for responding that were acknowledging of these experiences of trauma, but that did not run the risk of re-traumatising her.

These repositionings facilitated, for Millie, a distancing from the immediacy of aspects of her experience and from aspects of what was known and familiar to her about her life and her identity. These were aspects of her experience and of what was known and familiar to her that were significantly determined by and defined by the trauma of her history. In these repositionings, with support and encouragement, Millie was able to:

a) draw out relations between particular events and actions pertaining to the regulation of her bowels and to addressing traumatic experience,
b) reflect on these relations in the development of realisations and learnings about these phenomena,
c) abstract these realisations and learnings from concrete circumstances in the development of conclusions about life and identity, and
d) develop plans of action founded upon these realisations, and learnings, and conclusions.

Comment

I have proposed that Vygotsky's ideas about learning and development have the potential to contribute to understandings of therapeutic change generally, to lend clarity to what is significant in the conversations of narrative therapy, and to assist in the further development of narrative practices. And I have put forward his assertion about the social and relational origins of conceptual development and about this as a foundation of 'self-mastery' and 'self-regulation'. These considerations encourage us, as therapists, to acknowledge and honour the special responsibilities that we have to provide the conditions for the development of personal agency in the people who consult us.

Recognising that it is our task to scaffold the proximal zone of development in ways that support an incremental and progressive distancing from the known and familiar to what it is possible to know is an important aspect of acknowledging and honouring this responsibility. From this perspective, if a person's response to therapeutic inquiry is a not-knowing response: 'I don't know the answer to that'; 'I don't know how to respond to that', then our attention is drawn to the responsibilities that we have for the further scaffolding of these conversations. In observing these responsibilities we might drop down a level in the vertical dimension of our inquiry to give people the opportunity to further develop a reflecting surface that will enable them to respond to the next level of inquiry. Or we might provide opportunities for explorations of the horizontal dimension, perhaps by inviting others to speculate about appropriate responses to the questions of this inquiry, or by providing accounts of how others in similar predicaments have responded to such questions, and inviting reflection on this.

Another example of the special responsibilities that accompany this understanding of the therapeutic task: should we find ourselves falling prey to conclusions that a person who is consulting us is 'simply lacking motivation', is 'hopelessly irresponsible', is 'resistant', is 'incapable of foreseeing the consequences of his/her actions', is 'unable to reflect on his/her behaviour', is 'a concrete thinker', and/or is 'incapable of abstract thought', this will serve as a wake-up call. In observing these special responsibilities, we will interpret conclusions like these to be a reflection of the extent to which this person is mired in the known and familiar, and is not experiencing the sort of social collaboration that would be effective in scaffolding his/her zone of proximal development. In this circumstance, we are alerted to the fact that we have not been fully present with our scaffolding skills, or that we have reached the limits of these skills in our consultations with particular people in relation to specific issues. This second conclusion will encourage us to take pause to explore ways of extending on the limits of our therapeutic skills.

Conclusion

In this paper I have given three illustrations of therapeutic conversations with the families of young children in which externalising practices played a significant part. These externalising practices were also conceived as distancing practices that provided an opportunity for: Richard to distance from the ways that he had been defined by the problem; Gerry to distance from a principal known and familiar sense of his identity and for the rich development of a conception of personal strength; and for Millie to distance from traumatic experience and the ways in which this had defined her.

I provided a brief account of some of Lev Vygotsky ideas about early childhood learning, and drew out a 'scaffolding conversations' map for therapeutic conversations that was drawn from these ideas. Although Vygotsky's focus was on early childhood learning and development, I believe that the notion of the 'proximal zone of learning', and the importance given to the careful scaffolding of this zone, is relevant to all therapeutic conversations, regardless of the ages and stages of development of the people who are consulting therapists.

The accounts of my meetings with Richard and Jane, and with Gerry and his parents, were alternatively charted onto a 'statement of position map' and a 'scaffolding conversations' map. Space considerations only allowed for a partial illustration of the extent of the actual scaffolding of the therapeutic conversations according to these maps. This 'statement of position' map and this 'scaffolding conversations' map are constructions that were developed in the course of my consultations with people, and are not offered as imperatives in regard to the shaping of therapeutic conversations, or as claims about what is essential to adequate and appropriate therapeutic processes.

In the foregoing discussion, amongst other things, I have characterised therapeutic conversations that make it possible for people to traverse the space between the already known and familiar and what it is possible for them to know. I have invoked the notion of distancing to describe this process, and referred to the therapist's role in the scaffolding of this space. I have also emphasised that achieving what it is possible for one to know, and the sense of personal agency that is associated with this, is the outcome of social collaboration.

At the beginning of this paper I stated that it was my intention to review developments in my work with families with young children over more than twenty years, with the expectation that writing this chapter would provide an opportunity for me to re-visit and reflect on some of my therapeutic conversations with children over this time. I hope the stories about the therapeutic conversations included here give some sense of the playfulness, exuberance, laughter and tenderness that has characterised so many of my meetings with children and their families. Many of the practices that are now routinely associated with narrative therapy, including externalising conversations, were initially developed in the context of conversations with small children and their parents, siblings and/or care-givers. While this chapter has focused on the ways in which narrative practices can assist children to move beyond the known and familiar and towards what it is possible for them to know and do, it would be equally possible to write a chapter describing the contributions of children and their families to the development of this work, contributions that have assisted me to step beyond what was known and familiar to me in regard to my therapeutic practice. Perhaps there will be an opportunity to do so at a later date.

Note

This chapter began its life as a part of a presentation given at the Psychotherapy Networker Symposium in Washington in March 2003. This was a workshop that I co-presented with Salvador Minuchin, and it was planned with the intention that we would together review developments through different eras of the history of our work. We had agreed that videotape clips of meetings with families would provide the foundation for this review. I chose to focus on my work with families of young children, and in this chapter I refer to three of the stories that I shared in this presentation.

Reference

Vygotsky, L. 1986: *Thought and Language.* Cambridge: MIT Press.

CHAPTER TWO

The position of the therapist in working with children and their families

by Alice Morgan

Conversations with children in therapeutic contexts have given me great joy, energy and hope. There have also been times of dilemmas and complexities. In this chapter, I will share some stories from my counselling practice with children and their families that illustrate how many of these dilemmas, complexities and times of 'stuckness' have related to the question of the position of the therapist.

During therapeutic conversations, I am mindful of the differences in power between myself and the people with whom I am meeting. This is especially so in consultations with children. In meetings with children, the invitations for adults to reproduce dominant cultural practices of marginalisation are ever-present. This is true for all children by nature of their age and size, and is particularly true for some children more than others when experiences of gender, class, race, cultural background, are considered. In describing stories of my therapeutic practice with children, my intention is to explore carefully the responsibilities of therapists.

Throughout this paper I will reflect upon my positioning as a therapist. Whenever I've felt uneasy or unsettled about something that is occurring in a therapeutic conversation, when I've found it difficult to find ways of acting that fit with my preferences for my work with children, I have found it useful to consider how I am positioning myself in relation to the children consulting me[1].

Position of the therapist

Michael White has presented a diagram that shows four possible positions a therapist might hold in a therapeutic conversation (White 2005).

Decentred and Influential	*Centred and Non–Influential*
Decentred and Non-Influential	*Centred and Influential*

The position associated with narrative practice, and the position I prefer to remain in, is the Decentred and Influential position. This is a position where children's knowledges are honoured and the therapist uses their skills to structure contexts for the child's knowledges to become more richly described. Before providing examples of this position in practice, I will first look briefly at what the other three positions mean to me. I hope to draw some distinctions so that it is clearer and easier to think about the possible effects of each of these four therapeutic positions on the lives of children who consult us in therapy. I shall first consider the Centred and Influential position.

Centred and Influential Position

When therapists take up a centred and influential position, this privileges the knowledge and experience of the therapist. The experience of the child consulting the therapist is referenced against professional knowledge. The idea of the child as an authority on their own experience is likely to be less visible, and the expressions of the child are subject to interpretation according to particular professional discourses. In this position, the therapist role is associated with a (burden of) responsibility for independently fixing whatever the problem is, through their expert intervention.

This positioning privileges the knowledge and experience of the therapist over the local and particular knowledges of the child. In turn, the work becomes increasingly accountable to 'theories and principles that are considered to have universal relevance' (White 1997, p.200).

As a narrative therapist, I actively construct conversations with children in which the child is seen as the expert in his/her own life. There have been, however, various times in my practice when I have slipped into ways that are more centred; ways of being a therapist that position me more as the expert on the child's life. For instance, I've caught myself beginning to say or think: 'I think it would be good if ...' or 'you could ...' or I've started to think in terms of giving strategies, or offering steps to follow. Sometimes I've even felt a lecture coming on!

Over the years of my practice, I've noticed that the pull towards a more centred position seems stronger for me at certain times. A key factor in this seems to be if I've been meeting with a child for some time and they report that the influence of the problem is growing. I've also become aware that, for me, the younger the child and the greater the problem, the more I need to be mindful of ways to remain decentred.

Other times when I have found it hard to resist invitations to move toward a more centred and influential position in the therapeutic context include when a child takes a step that seems to me to be a positive one. In these circumstances, if I were to offer my congratulations or praise rather than seek to know what these steps had meant to the child, my values and beliefs would become centred in the conversation. It's even possible for my congratulatory comments to have the effect of being understood as a judgement reflecting what is important to me[2].

These are, however, relatively easy slip-ups for me to spot. It was more complicated the day I met with Alex and his family.

Alex and his family

Alex, who is five years old, consulted me about the 'Wizzies' that were taking up lots of his time and concentration at school. Alex, his family and I had been meeting over a four week period, exposing the many tricks, tactics and intentions of the 'Wizzies' in the life of the family. We had a developing appreciation of Alex's views on the Wizzies (that he didn't like them) and what Alex wanted for his life. Alex had made many attempts to catch the Wizzies into his pencil case and had made many elaborate devices from Lego[3] to assist him with his pursuits. He figured that if he put them in his pencil case they could still be his friend but not get him into so much trouble or steer his life off track.

At our fifth meeting, all the family (including Alex) reported that things were worse. The Wizzies were bigger and the Lego devices didn't work. Alex's parents said they were wondering if the therapy was 'working' and that Alex's teacher was getting 'towards the end of her tether'. Alex's teacher had told the parents she intended to introduce a sticker chart system (behaviour modification) in the classroom and had asked for their support.

In this example, many of the key adults in Alex's life were being influenced by ideas that were less appealing to me. They were expressing interest in ways of helping Alex that seemed more about centring adults' ideas about what might address the effects of the problem. These included giving Alex positive reinforcement for good behaviour at school and demonstrating to him the 'consequences' of bad behaviour.

I was distressed to hear the family report what they'd noticed about the Wizzies. I felt sad that the Wizzies were being so bothersome and hadn't got the message as yet. Distress and concern invited me to start thinking ... 'What else can we try?' and: 'Is there a way we could use stickers in the classroom to turn things around? What can I suggest?'

I stopped myself. I sat back a moment and tried to re-align myself in the conversation more to a position of enquiry. I tried to recall the voices and experiences of other children I'd met with to help me – the memories of stories I had heard from other children who had had to deal with experiences of problems getting bigger. I thought of all the successes, the richness of this work and the effects on the lives of those children now. This helped to orient me back to using the maps of narrative therapy that centred Alex's views and knowledges.

I started by saying something like: 'From what you've been telling me, the Wizzies seem to be getting bigger and taking up more space than you all want. Is that right?' They all agreed. 'So when this is happening, how does this have you thinking about yourselves? Or about your hopes for the future?'

Alex said that it made him feel like a 'loser' and that the Wizzies were so naughty that he wondered lately if they might be around forever. He said this would be bad for his life because he liked to do Game Boy (an electronic game) and if the Wizzies stayed around forever he wouldn't be able to concentrate on this. Alex's parents said that when the Wizzies were making a 'comeback' (these were the words they used to describe what was going on) it had them feeling like failures as parents and had them considering giving up. Alex said that it had him feeling like giving up too. They all said they didn't like this 'giving up feeling' because it meant that they weren't as happy.

I said, 'This comeback of the Wizzies seems to be getting in the way of some things that are important to you as a family? Have I understood you correctly?' They unanimously agreed.

'Yes', said Alex's mum, 'I can't believe it because we've always been a family who sticks together when things get tough'. This statement caught my attention as it seemed to indicate a history of knowledge, and experience of what to do 'when things get tough' that intrigued me.

I began to ask lots of questions about the history of the commitment to 'stick together in tough times'. For example:

- How many generations would this commitment go back?
- Who first started it do you think?
- Did you, Alex, know about this as something in your family?
  What is it like to hear this?
- Who else would know about this?

These conversations articulated a richer description of particular family members who had contributed to this commitment continuing through the generations. I heard many stories that fitted with this theme. I heard about how Alex's grandfather, who was most loved and adored by Alex, never gave up when he was recovering from his recent heart surgery. I heard how Alex never gave up when he was learning to ride a bike. I heard how Alex's dad almost gave up trying to learn yoga, but has kept going. I heard about how Alex's aunty never gives up when she's eating icecream – even if she's really full and can't take one more mouthful!

These were just a few examples of some of the stories that were told. The re-authoring[4] and re-membering[5] conversations we engaged in, provided a richer description for the family that they said 'cast new light' on the current 'comeback' of the Wizzies. They all said they felt a lot stronger after the conversation. They spoke of renewed determination to ensure that the participation of the Wizzies in the family occurred on the family's terms, not on the Wizzies' terms. They also left with a few new ideas for the coming days - ways to keep the family legacy closer to them during this 'tough time'. This, they said, was very helpful and they were pleased about it.

Remaining decentred made a big difference to Alex and his family. We met three more times, after which the family reported our meetings were no longer necessary as Alex now had the Wizzies back where he wanted them. There were a few setbacks in this progress three months later, however, two more meetings, as Alex put it, 'set things straight again'.

I notice myself slipping toward a Centred and Influential position as a therapist when I ask a question that is phrased in such a way to be likely to elicit a particular answer that I have in mind, or when I ask a question in a way that implies the answer. I prefer to ask questions that leave room for children to make meaning of their experiences. This is not always such an easy thing to do, as I discovered the day I met with Jason and his family.

Renee, Jose and Jason

It was a crisp spring morning in October when Jason, who is eleven years old, and his adopted parents, Renee and Jose, came to meet with me. The conversations we had shared previously were at the request of Renee and Jose on account of Jason's refusal to go to school. Jose and Renee said at our first meeting that they thought this was about 'Jason's inability to cope with his adoption and the family breakdown'. His older brother had recently moved out of the house to live independently under circumstances that caused them a 'great heartache'. Jason had told us he thought that Renee and Jose's ideas on the problem were all 'bullshit' and that he was okay and just didn't like school.

Whilst I wanted to remain respectful of the meanings Jose and Renee had made of Jason's life, I was mindful of working in ways that centred Jason's knowledges and supported some alternative or preferred descriptions of him that they all might find useful. During the course of our first few meetings, many narrative practices supported me to remain in a decentred and influential position until this day in October when things went a bit astray!

In our previous meetings, we had made progress in (according to the family) considering some of the things that were important to Jason. Jason had spoken of his hope to one day be a mechanic or a football player because he said 'life should be about living, not sitting around being bored'. This theme of 'life being about living' became a focus for many interesting discussions in which I enquired about stories and events from his earlier life that were linked with these principles.

On this particular morning, Renee arrived and seemed particularly excited, eager to tell me about a 'really good thing that Jason has done'. Renee told me that Jason had been to school and kicked a goal in football. Overtaken by the spirit in which Renee offered this story, and knowing that Jason had not attended school for twelve days straight, I quickly began asking him more about this event, assuming that it was a unique and sparkling development to him. I started asking questions to place this event into the story of 'life being about living'. For example:

- when you played footy that day, did that fit or not fit with 'life being about living'?
- How did you get ready to take that step?
- What led up to it? What thinking supported you to do what you did?

Lucky for me, Jason immediately noticed my slip in positioning. He was quick to say: 'That's no big deal. I wish you'd all stop going on about it'. Without Jason's reminder, perhaps my enthusiasm might have got to the point of actively trying to convince him that kicking the footy was a unique outcome! Instead, I quickly apologised for my assumptions and asked where he thought we should begin for the day. Jason said: 'Well, can I ask you a question?'

'Of course', I replied. Jason reached for his father's mobile phone, tapped away at some of the keys and asked 'do you know what that is?' This is what was on the screen :-) I said I thought that if you turned the screen horizontally, it was a smiley face. Jason smiled, said: 'Cool', and proceeded to return a text message to someone. I very cautiously and hesitantly asked him if would be okay to ask who he was sending the message to.

Jason said: 'Yeah, sure, it's just Rick, someone in the footy team'. A subsequent thorough enquiry revealed that, unbeknown to Jose and Renee, Rick and Jason had sent a few text messages to each other since the day Jason had scored the goal in the footy match. The more I asked about this, the more

Jason was keen to tell me what it meant to him. Jason thought that it was to do with 'being ready to make a few friends again, not wanting to be alone so much'. Jason considered this to be a significant development and one he told me he'd been thinking about for a few months. Had I not been careful, this initiative may have been lost and the potential for engaging Jason in many re-authoring conversations missed.

As Jason was giving me the specific details about his intentions for his life, Renee and Jose listened. They explained that the tears they shed as they did so were tears of relief, of surprise and of hope.

It would have been very easy, had I not been mindful of placing Jason's knowledge at the centre of the work, to follow Renee's interest and excitement, thereby placing her knowledge or preferences at the centre of the conversation. The information that Renee had offered about the goal at football was highly relevant to our meeting and her sharing this played a significant part in alerting us all to potential story development. Looking back, however, if I had continued with my assumption that the footy goal was a key development to Jason, the opportunities to hear of his newfound friendship, and intentions for friendship, would have been lost.

Centred and Non-Influential

There are a range of ways in which therapists can take up a centred and yet non-influential position. In these circumstances, the therapist's knowledge and meanings are still privileged but their influence in the conversation is minimal. For instance, perhaps the therapist is taking more of a listening role in the session but is actively interpreting what is being said according to a set of professional knowledges.

The therapist's intention is to remain neutral so as not to 'contaminate' or influence what the person consulting them says or thinks.

While I am not likely to simply sit and listen during a session, there are times in my practice when I find myself taking a more centred and yet non-influential position. If I lead a conversation towards what is of importance or greatest interest to me, assuming that this is just as important to the person at the centre, and then discover that the conversation goes nowhere, this is an instance of taking a centred and yet non-influential position. The times when I am most likely to choose a direction in the conversation without checking if it is of interest to the child, are when I meet with a child whose experiences resonate with the experiences of other children with whom I have met. When a child, for example, begins telling me about the 'mean tricks' the other children in his class were subjecting him to, I try to remind myself to enquire about their experience in such a way that I haven't heard before, rather than being eager to tell the child that I've spoken to lots of other children about teasing and stepping too quickly away from the particularities of their story.

When I assume I know what a child means when they use particular language, or when I leap ahead of them, it seems as though things just 'go over people's heads', like they've taken no notice, or are more captured in their own thinking than in my inquiry. For example, they might look as if they've tuned out or stopped listening, or their eyes might glaze over as though they are at a loss to understand what I might have just said or asked. From what I've noticed, when this happens, the outcome is that I am centred but non-influential; they are able to quickly disregard or fob things off as meaningless to them. I assume this is because what I have said or asked is irrelevant, disconnected or distant from their own particular experiences. At these moments I am grateful that children usually let me know pretty quickly that things have gone off track, and I try to reorient myself to a more preferable position!

Max, Aliga and Henry

I can think of various times in my practice when I've contributed to making the meaning of events for people rather than inviting children to make meaning from the stories they are telling. One time I recall this happening was when Max, Aliga, Henry and I were meeting because they wanted to talk about how their fathers lived in separate houses from their mothers. I found our meetings particularly lively although I often found it difficult to engage as much energy for bouncing around in the room as they did!

One day, in a careless attempt to name some developments that they were speaking about, I asked 'So, would you say that when you did that, it means you're boys who value people who do things a bit differently than the usual?' These words were my words and an interpretation of what Aliga had said. My interpretation was based on something that is important to me in my life. It was also the type of question for which I was hoping for a particular answer (that is Yes!). I'm grateful to Aliga for setting me on a more productive path by looking bemused, disinterested and saying: 'Nup. I dunno'.

Louisa

Making assumptions about what a person means when they use particular language is another practice associated with taking a centred non-influential position. My conversations with Louisa (11 years) taught me about the importance of asking children about the meanings that they give to particular words and phrases they use.

Louisa was consulting me about the sadness she felt about her mother's recent diagnosis of breast cancer. Her mum had 'a few months left for living' and Louisa said she was now 'doing lots of cramming with her mum'. I assumed that 'cramming' meant that Louisa was doing lots of different activities with her mum in a short space of time. This is what the word cramming means to me. I therefore asked her: 'What will you and your mum be cramming in?' In response, Louisa looked bemused. So, I took a step back and asked: 'What did you mean when you said 'cramming'?'

Louisa explained: 'Oh cramming is when we just lie around doing nuthin' ...'

I soon learnt that this term was one that had been affectionately used for many generations in Lousa's family. Louisa said it was like 'chilling out', 'time out' , 'vegging'. If I had not asked more questions about this phrase, I would have missed a valuable opportunity to acknowledge the significance and uniqueness of this way of being with her mother and how it was linked to certain family traditions and stories.

Leaping ahead of people also runs the risk of being in a centred non-influential position. In my experience, there are lots of ways this can happen! For instance, coming up with ideas about what people might do next that have nothing to do with what they've said the next steps might be.

Decentred and Non-influential

I think of the decentred and non-influential position as a standing back position, almost an 'anything goes' kind of approach. The intention is to centre the person's experience and meaning and yet, when taking a decentred and non-influential position, the therapist becomes passive and the responsibility for influence over the direction of therapy is minimised.

Taking a decentred and non-influential position in therapeutic conversations results in focusing on the meanings and preferences of the person coming to therapy without any consideration of the responsibility of the therapist for what happens in these conversations. This could, however, be fraught in a number of ways. For instance:

- What would it mean if, as a therapist, I didn't interrupt when I noticed I was hearing ongoing re-tellings of the problem story in ways that seemed to be furthering division or distress?
- What would it mean if I remained silent in situations in therapy in which an adult or adults minimise, disregard or disrespect a child's wishes? If I remain silent at these times, what does this mean that I am colluding with?
- Similarly, what are the effects if I disregard moments in which the discourses of homophobia enter conversations with children, for example if a child says: 'Oh that's so gay' in a derogatory way in the course of a therapeutic conversation?
- Alternatively, when a child tells me that he or she likes hitting and kicking, where do my responsibilities lie?

There are many times during therapeutic consultations when as therapists, we are required to think through and respond to complexities that relate to the politics of experience. At these times, taking a non-influential position would have considerable effects – including colluding with marginalising practices. I will now share a story to illustrate this.

Making choices

Some years ago I wrote about a number of conversations I had with groups of children who were using teasing and bullying to persecute their peers[6]. At the time, I was working as a school counsellor receiving referrals to see children from teachers, parents and children themselves. Amy was referred to me by her teacher. The teacher told me that Amy had been bullied and that she hoped I might help her to feel better about herself and what had happened.

At this point, Amy's distress had been noted by the school and by her parents who, out of their care and love for their daughter, had sought assistance for Amy. They hoped that counselling might assist her in relation to enhancing her self-esteem and resilience. This is why she had been referred to me. Up until then, the focus had remained on Amy. No-one had considered the idea of holding those responsible more accountable for their actions. Whilst I was open to the idea of seeing Amy in therapy, I also spent a considerable amount of time talking with the school community about the importance of working not just with the effects of abuse but more importantly with those who were responsible for it. This idea was influential in contributing to a shift in thinking in the school. As well as providing support for victims, we began to focus attention also on the group of girls who were doing the teasing. Amy became a consultant to this work – I met with her to see if she felt things were improving or slipping back, and about the effects of my work with the girls who had been tormenting her. These are often referred to as practices of accountability.

What might I have contributed to if I did not attempt to respond to those who were enacting the bullying? What were the likely effects on Amy if the problem was individualised and located 'within' Amy as an issue of lack of self-esteem or resilience? The role of therapist involves making many important decisions. I think we have the responsibility to use the power of our role in influential ways.

Decentred and Influential

A decentred and influential position is one that fits with my preferences for work with children and families. This orientation sees the person or family as the expert in their own lives, and places the knowledges, skills, preferences and commitments of the family at the centre of the work. In this position, the therapist plays a very active and critical role. The therapist is influential, not in the sense of setting the agenda for the meeting, but through skilfully scaffolding questions and responses in ways that enable the skills and knowledges of the child and family to become more richly known, so that these can be put to work to address current predicaments.

For me, this is a positioning that takes into account the power relations that significantly shape people's experience – in relation to gender, age, race, sexual preference, class, physical size, knowledge, etc. It is a position that acknowledges that the therapist is not separate from the influence of these discourses and that our work involves making visible the effects of these discourses.

In this position the therapist is not neutral. We have responsibilities to notice the power we have, acknowledge our influence, and reflect on the effects of this power and influence on the lives of others.

When I meet with children and the adults who care for them, I assume that the problems for which they are consulting me are in some way making it difficult for them to connect with their skills and preferences for living. The preferred and alternative stories of their lives and relationships are less visible under the weight of the dominant problem-saturated descriptions they bring to therapy. Through listening and asking questions in particular ways, I seek to bring forward these alternative and preferred knowledges, to facilitate contexts where the alternative stories of their lives are told and retold so they may be more richly known and available.

I know that this rich description will not happen by chance. As a therapist, I play a critical role in constructing contexts that make such rich description possible. I consider this decentred but influential position to require expertise, skill and rigour.

I have found that the practice maps of narrative therapy developed by Michael White provide ways for me to remain decentred and influential. Remembering conversations, outsider-witness practices, taking-it-back practices, transparency, re-authoring conversations, and practices of acknowledgement, are all ways that support me to remain decentred with children consulting me[7]. These practices have all been useful ways for me to keep children's skills and knowledges at the centre of the conversations we share, and at the same time keep me decentred. These maps of practice support my intentions in the work.

The families who have consulted me in the past have helped me to be clearer on how I can use my influence to provide the sorts of contexts that will contribute to thickening the preferred stories of children's identities. I value their contribution to my thinking on this. I'd like to share some examples from my practice and hope they illustrate what I consider to be the complex nature of this decentred influential position, the responsibilities that flow from it, and the inevitable dilemmas and complications I've found myself grappling with.

Joining Externalising conversations

Talking about problems in ways that separate them from people is a linguistic practice that opens space for alternative descriptions of children to emerge and for children's preferred stories to become more available to them. I have found that many children are able to quickly step into these sorts of conversations. What happens, though, when an adult care-giver in the room is slower to join with externalising language, or seeks to actively direct the conversation back to help me understand what is really wrong or deficient with their child?

I regard these sorts of responses from adults as completely understandable given the dominant western cultural discourses that are so pervasive and which powerfully locate problems as within people. There are many popular ideas that locate problems as people, that invite parents or the adults who care for the child to feel either shame or blame when things go wrong, and which position therapists as experts who can diagnose problems and provide the 'treatment' or cure. The idea that we need to look at the cause of problems in order to fix them is another that circulates widely. I've therefore come to expect that it may be quite an adjustment for some adults to step into externalising language when I first meet with them. These situations raise some questions for me.

- How can I respond during therapeutic conversations to ways of speaking that describe the child as the problem?
- How can I use my influence to support different sorts of tellings from adults?

I can think of many different ways I've tried to manage these situations in the past. One way I have found helpful is to talk with parents or other relevant adults before I meet with the child or children. A phone conversation, or face-to-face meeting, can lay the foundations to invite them into collaboration and as co-authors in the work we are about to embark on together. Within these preparatory conversations, I explain that I may begin the conversations with the child without mentioning or focussing on the problem. I explain that I will be trying to get a sense of their child's identity separate from the problem. In preparatory conversations I may also ask the adult(s) what they know about their child's skills, abilities and what they appreciate about them, or consider special or unique.

I sometimes also explain a little bit about externalising conversations and then ask a range of questions including:

- What do you think of the idea that the problem is the problem and that the person is not the problem? Do you think it will support your child's life to see it in that way? How might this affect your view of yourselves as parents, teachers, foster carers, to see this as separate from you all?
- How will it be for you that I will be focusing on making visible the skills and knowledges your child has for his/her life? How does that fit or not fit with your beliefs as parents/workers/carers, etc? How do you think your child will respond?
- In what ways do you hope you can join with your child/ren against the influence of the problem?

Within these preparatory conversations I may also speak openly about discourses of 'mother-blame' and discuss how I am interested in deconstructing this.

After explaining a bit about my approach to counselling, I might then interview the parents/care-givers (using the maps of narrative practice) about what they've heard. This enquiry deliberately seeks out stories about what is important to the adults in the care of their child, and their preferred ways of being a parent, teacher, carer, etc. This often provides fertile ground for rich story development that can then be referred to and built upon in future therapeutic conversations in which the child is present.

If it seems relevant, I may also offer some articles to the adults about narrative practice, or show them examples of therapeutic documents that other children have given their permission to share.

Finally, I will ask the parents/care-givers if they wish to go ahead and give this process a try. I then ensure that there will be an ongoing structure to consult with them at set periods to hear about how the process is going for them and to discuss any questions or dilemmas they may have along the way. I then offer to send a letter to the child to introduce myself and invite them to meet me. And we go from there.

There are also other ways I've found to be influential in supporting and inviting parents/care-givers to join with me in this work. I consider finding ways to invite others to join our conversations as collaborative partners an important element in being influential in this work.

Making space for rich story development

Another time that I have found it useful to reflect on how I can purposefully use my influence in this work is when adults in the room are taking up more of the talking than the children who are present. This sort of situation raises many questions for me:

- If I allow adults to take up more space than children, what is this saying about what I think of children's knowledges?
- If adults do a majority of the telling and speaking, where is it likely to

invite them to stand in relation to the child and the problem? Will it be more likely to contribute to them feeling more or less responsible for the problem?

- What other discourses might I be reproducing by not interrupting this? What discourses might I need to watch out to not reproduce if I do interrupt?
- If the context of society is such that children are rarely consulted about their preferences for their lives, how might my conversations with children offer something different?

In work with children, my intention is to give children space to speak and be consulted. When significant adults in the life of the child are present, my hope is to do this in close collaboration with them, and not in opposition to them.

I am hoping to illustrate this sort of collaboration through an example of when Janet and Matthew consulted with me.

Matthew and Janet

Janet called me concerned about her nine-year-old son, Matthew, who had been injured in an accident at school about eighteen months previously. This accident left him with a significant disability. The movement on the right side of his body was restricted and his fine motor co-ordination affected. Matthew was 'devastated' that he could no longer play soccer in the soccer team and couldn't ride his skateboard like he used to. Janet said that the accident was very distressing to her also. She had made many changes to accommodate for the level of care Matthew now required; she'd reduced the time she spent in paid work, now saw less of her friends, and said she wasn't sure what else she could do to help Matthew.

Janet was ringing to enquire about help for Matthew. She described Matthew's behaviour as 'out of control' at home, he had low self-esteem, he 'wasn't coping with the disability', and often referred to himself as 'stupid and useless'. Janet told me she hoped I might be able to help Matthew feel better about himself: 'He used to be such a happy-go-lucky type of kid and I think if we don't do something about it now it will just scar him for life'. Janet said that Matthew's father was 'no longer in the picture' and she wondered if his behaviour had something to do with that also. Janet was obviously very worried for Matthew and said she would do anything to assist him in dealing with their new circumstances.

In this conversation, before engaging with Matthew, I spent some time enquiring about Janet's views on the problem, her opinions on Matthew's qualities that she appreciated, and her hopes and intentions for the therapy. We had a conversation around the themes that I mentioned earlier in relation to how I work and the many different ways we might construct our meetings. I mentioned, for example, that at times I might see Matthew alone, see Janet alone, see them together, and even invite other people to come along as well.

Janet shared stories with me about some of the history of her preferences in parenting. She said she had always wanted to support Matthew to express his feelings and that she was concerned that Matthew simply 'wouldn't talk' to her about anything lately. This was the cause of much distress to Janet and she wanted some help with getting him to 'open up to her'.

In our conversation together we also explored how the problem had been affecting her. We discovered that it had been inviting her to increase her efforts in relation to Matthew, having her do more for him than she preferred. She also said that since the problem had been around she often compared herself to other mothers and that the dominant messages from society about what constituted success as a mother had been inviting her to thinking she was a failure. Janet explained she had tried a number of different things at home already to help Matthew. These efforts she evaluated to be varied in their degrees of success.

Reading Matthew a story before he went to sleep and sitting on his bed until he drifted off to sleep had sometimes given them space to talk in ways they both enjoyed. Janet had also tried to boost his self-esteem by trying to notice all the times when he was doing the right thing, rather than the bad behaviour. This she said was a challenge, but that Matthew seemed to respond better to praise than punishment. Since the difficulties, Janet had also read a number of self-help books and talked to her friends who offered some support and sympathy for what she was going through. This she said had kept her going. 'It's my love for him', she said: 'He's just so special to me'. Through these conversations Janet explained that what was most important to her was to see Matthew happy again, for him to talk to her, and for the amount of conflict in the house to reduce.

My intention throughout was to put Janet's knowledges about Matthew at the centre; to centre her skills, abilities and preferences as a mother. Before we concluded, I checked with Janet if it would be okay to interview her further about her ideas once I had met Matthew. Janet said she would like that as she had enjoyed our conversation. Janet said Matthew would be willing to meet me so I sent him a letter before we met.

Dear Matthew,

Hi! My name is Alice. I spoke to your mum on the phone today and she said it would be okay to send you this letter. I talk with lots of people about what's going on in their lives and they tell me some pretty interesting things. Your mum told me that you've had to get used to some new things lately. I'm guessing you know a bit about what it takes to get used to things, especially when they don't seem fair? Your mum also told me that you love computer games and are really good at helping out in the library at school. I'd love to know more about your collection of nature cards too, if you'd like to bring them along.

I look forward to meeting you, Alice.

In our first meeting Janet and Matthew came along. Here is a snapshot from our conversation.

Matthew: Yeah, and in the library I get to do some of the stuff on the computer. Mrs Gennings lets me.

Alice: Mrs Gennings lets you and not the other kids?

Matthew: Yeah.

Alice: How come do you reckon?

Janet: Well, Matthew is very reliable aren't you Matthew?

Matthew: (Silent)

Alice: Okay. So, can I just ask you Matthew a bit more about the library thing ...?

Matthew: Yes.

Alice: Well you said that Mrs Gennings lets you ... How come? What do you think she sees in you or knows about you that would tell her it's okay for you to go on the computer?

Janet: Well, since the accident, Matthew has spent lots of time in the library so Mrs Gennings knows him pretty well.

Alice: So Matthew what do you think about that?

Matthew: I ...

Janet: Well, Matthew used to be such a friendly kid, he always was, since he was really little ... but not now, since the accident ... have you Matthew? Tell Alice how you cry all the time now and how you've told me you hate yourself.

In this conversation, Janet responded a number of times on Matthew's behalf and then directed the conversation away from the preferred and alternative stories of Matthew that were beginning to emerge, and toward the problem story.

This was a tricky situation to find myself in, but not uncommon. It felt tricky as I was holding many considerations at the same time. I was juggling many complex thoughts.

I was aware of the importance of not diminishing in any way what Janet had shared with me about some of the effects of the problem on her life, and I wanted to pay attention to the pressures she may have been under as a mother of a child whose abilities had changed so significantly. Staying close to thinking about how discourses of the dominant culture might be contributing to how Janet's responses were shaped, and finding ways to begin deconstructing those ideas, were also in my mind. I hoped that in my response I could offer support to Janet and wondered if I could in some way explore what may have been 'absent but implicit' (White 2000) in Janet speaking on Matthew's behalf. Could it be, for example, that Janet's responses fitted with the commitments she held for finding ways for Matthew to express himself? Or for her intentions in helping Matthew to express what she appreciated or knew Matthew was capable of?

At the same time, however, I wanted to respond in ways that would consult Matthew and centre his knowledges.

On this particular occasion, I asked Janet if it would be okay to ask Matthew some questions for a bit. She agreed. I turned to Matthew and asked his permission to ask him a few questions. He said he was willing and proceeded to tell me some more about being in the library.

He told me that he did all the borrowing and returning of the books in the library and that he liked using the scanner on the computer to do it. After a while I asked him about his views on coming to see me. Did he think it was a good or not so good idea? Matthew jubilantly said it was 'okay' and he thanked me for the letter. Matthew thought the letter was 'good' because he liked getting letters. I told Matthew that his mum thought it would be good to talk to help him deal with the things going on in his life at the moment. Matthew nodded.

Alice: What do you think of the idea of us talking a bit about what's going on for you at the moment, 'cos your mum told me that you thought that things in life can seem pretty unfair sometimes. Is that right?

Matthew: Yes, because in our class at school you're not allowed to use pen in your books until you've got a pen license.

Matthew's comment led to a longer conversation about his knowledge of things that seem unfair. Matthew thought it was unfair, for example, that some people in the world didn't have a home and lived on the streets. He also thought that kids teasing other kids was unfair, and that what had happened to him was unfair.

I asked Matthew what he thought would be helpful for us to spend time talking about. Matthew didn't know, but said that we'd made an okay start and that he'd like to come back another day to show me his nature cards.

Future conversations focused around Matthew's interest in turning the volume down on the Mean Voices that were making his life hard. The Mean Voices told him he was stupid and dumb, that no-one liked him, and got him into lots of arguing with his mum. Matthew and his mum said they both thought the Mean Voices were out for trouble . They wanted the Mean Voices to be put back in their places before they made any more trouble.

Articulating Matthew's abilities in knowing fairness from unfairness provided the opening for many re-authoring conversations about what Matthew stood for in life. This included: 'Standing for giving everyone a turn', 'Not being mean' and 'Helping out others'. In time, these themes were traced and linked with actions in the current and past events of his life.

The scope of this paper means that I won't be able to go into a full description of where the therapy with Matthew went after this. However, I do want to return to the key role that Janet played in this work. As re-authoring conversations with Matthew evolved, Janet began to act as a vital outsider witness[8] to the stories of his life. This fitted with her intentions and preferences as a parent and it provided invaluable support in thickening Matthew's preferred themes for his life. I used a structure that I hoped would:

- enable Matthew's knowledges and skills to remain at the centre of our conversations,
- provide avenues for Janet to be engaged as a very important witness and co-author for the preferred stories of Matthew's life,

- enable both Janet's and Matthew's intentions and hopes for the therapy to shape the focus of the consultations,
- decentre me in the process.

The structures that developed involved me sometimes meeting with Matthew on his own. Matthew was happy to do this and we talked about ways we would catch his mum up on what we'd talked about. When I met with Matthew, I videotaped the conversation (with his permission) and Matthew then chose the parts of the conversation he thought would be important to share with his mum.

At times I met with Janet on her own. In these meetings we continued developing the themes she had spoken about in our initial conversation: about what was important to her as a parent. Janet's intentions, commitments, principles, hopes and beliefs became more richly described in these consultations. In one of these meetings, Janet said that Matthew 'being his own person' was important to her as a parent. These re-authoring conversations about her parenting helped to re-connect Janet with her preferred ways of being which she said had been hard to hold onto since Matthew's accident.

I shared the video clips of the conversations with Matthew and consulted Janet about how she thought the therapeutic process was going for Matthew and for herself. I wanted to know if what was happening was fitting or not fitting with her initial hopes for our meetings. She said she saw some positive changes in Matthew and she wished the meetings to continue. She told me she felt 'less of a burden' and was finding things easier at home.

After a number of these individual meetings, Matthew, Janet and I then met together again. This time around, Janet said early on that she wanted to give Matthew lots of time to talk and say things because she was discovering things she never knew about that were pleasing to her.

When I interviewed Matthew, I continued to seek out rich descriptions of the alternative stories of his life. These included the stories Matthew had about his life being 'for fairness', about his abilities in the library and as the soccer score person. These also included a story about Matthew's 'mature thinking' that was helping him handle 'not seeing his dad anymore,' and stories about the discoveries Matthew was making about the Mean Voices and the ways he was managing to 'get on top of them'.

In some of these conversations Janet listened to our conversation, either sitting in the same room or from behind a one-way screen. Other times she watched videotapes we made of Matthew speaking. In each of these different circumstances I interviewed Janet about what seemed significant to her in the things Matthew had said. I asked what images this evoked for her about what Matthew gave value to in his life. I asked about why these particular things stood out for her, and then asked her about what difference hearing these things would make for her. These questions were guided by the categories of questions developed by Michael White for outsider-witness practice[9].

I also involved Janet by asking her to contribute further stories that fitted with some of the themes Matthew had begun to talk about. For example, in one of our videotaped meetings that Janet witnessed, Matthew said that it was important to him to: 'Be close to people and to have lots of fun'. At my next opportunity, I interviewed Janet in relation to what she knew about this. Janet confirmed that Matthew always has fun at birthday parties and that she knew other kids invited him to their parties because he cracked jokes and made them laugh. Janet also told stories about what she had seen Matthew doing that she thought were examples of him getting on top of the Mean Voices. We found ways to ensure that Matthew was an audience to these stories of Janet's. In this way, her stories contributed to thickening accounts of Matthew's preferred values. This process centred Matthew in the conversations and provided avenues for Janet's unique knowledges as his mother to support rich story development.

Over the course of our meetings I also found ways to engage other children to act as outsider witnesses to Matthew's stories. I invited Matthew to attend a group for kids where these children shared their stories together. This was another way of being influential by providing a particular structure that would keep children's know-how at the centre of consultations.

When our meetings were drawing to a close, I asked both Matthew and Janet about the current status of the issues and problems they had initially sought help with. Janet commented on how she no longer felt to blame for what had happened and she had realised that Matthew could manage. She said that when they first came, she and Matthew were arguing all the time, and didn't 'see eye-to-eye' on things. She reported that things were now 'a lot better'. Janet thought Matthew was coping a lot better and seemed happier in himself. Matthew had recently asked a friend over to their house which Janet considered a good sign. She also said that it had been important to her to have someone join with her in her hope for giving Matthew more of a say about what was happening in his life. Matthew confirmed that these meetings had made a difference in his life. He said: 'They've helped me a lot (to realise that) ... I'm not dumb ... Things are going to be different now 'cause my arms don't work as well, but that's not so bad ...' Matthew said that the stories his mum told about him were funny and interesting and that the Mean Voices were now easier to manage and to ignore. He said this meant he felt happier and that he now had things to look forward to in life.

In this work, I was active and deliberate in the ways in which I structured the conversations so that Matthew's skills and knowledge were centred. I did not leave this to chance, nor assume it was something that could be achieved without my influence. There are many different ways of working collaboratively with children and their families. This has just been one example[10].

Conclusion

In this chapter, I've reflected on four possible positions a therapist can take in therapeutic consultations and have shared some stories with you about the joyful work that I have experienced with children and their families. I hope these stories have illustrated some of the ways I've found to remain in a decentred and influential position, and some of the ways I have sought to get back on track when I've found myself in positions in which I am uncomfortable. In my experience, the decentred influential position makes it possible to have collaborative conversations with children and their families. This is a collaboration that centres children as the experts on their own lives. It is also a form of collaboration that is attentive to the politics of therapeutic work. And, for me, this combination keeps the work alive and inspiring.

Notes

1. The focus of this paper is specifically on work with children, however, I consider the discussion relating to the positioning of the therapist to be relevant to other therapeutic contexts.
2. As an alternative to forms of therapist acknowledgement that centre the therapist's values and interpretations, 'taking-it-back practices' are decentred and yet influential ways of responding to developments in people's lives. For more information about 'taking-it-back practices' see White (1997).
3. Plastic construction toy.
4. For more information about re-authoring conversations see Morgan (2000) and Russell & Carey (2005).
5. For more information about re-membering conversations see Morgan (2000) and Russell & Carey (2005).
6. To read about this approach to teasing and bullying in schools see Morgan (1995).
7. There are many examples in this book of these narrative practices. For more information see Morgan (2000) and Russell & Carey (2005). For examples of the use of these practices with children see Freeman, Epston & Lobovits (1997).
8. For more information about outsider-witness practices see Chapter 4 of this book and White (2004).
9. For more information about these categories of questions, see Chapter 4 of this book and White (2004).
10. To read of other options for collaborative conversations with children/young people and their families, see Chapter 5 of this book.

References

Freeman, J., Epston, D. & Lobovits, D. 1997: *Playful Approaches to Serious Problems: Narrative therapy with children and their families.* New York: WW Norton.

Morgan, A. 1995: 'Taking responsibility: Working with teasing and bullying in schools.' *Dulwich Centre Newsletter*, Nos. 2&3.

Morgan, A. 2000: *What is Narrative Therapy? An easy-to-read introduction.* Adelaide: Dulwich Centre Publications.

Russell, S. & Carey, M. (eds) 2004: *Narrative Therapy: Responding to your questions.* Adelaide: Dulwich Centre Publications.

White, M. 1997: *Narratives of Therapists' Lives.* Adelaide: Dulwich Centre Publications.

White, M. 2000: 'Re-engaging with history: The absent but implicit'. *Reflections on Narrative Practice.* Adelaide: Dulwich Centre Publications.

White, M. 2004: 'Working with people who have suffered the consequences of multiple trauma.' *International Journal of Narrative Therapy and Community Work, No.1.*

White, M. 2005: 'Workshop notes'. *www.dulwichcentre.com.au* Updated 21st September.

CHAPTER THREE

Responding to children who have experienced significant trauma: a narrative perspective

an interview with Michael White

When working with children who have experienced significant trauma, what are some of the key considerations?

In talking with children about experiences of trauma, safety is always the first consideration. Many of the children with whom we work may be experiencing ongoing trauma, or be living in physically unsafe contexts. Workers will be familiar with the importance of giving priority to addressing issues of physical and emotional safety in children's lives. There are also considerations of safety that are entirely pertinent to how we speak with children about experiences of trauma. Unless we take significant care in how we speak with children about experiences of trauma, we can inadvertently re-traumatise them. The identity of children who have been through significant trauma is often defined by this trauma, and if we invite children to speak about this trauma without first assisting them to find a different territory of identity on which to stand, this can be re-traumatising. There are a range of narrative practices that enable conversations about trauma to take place without re-traumatising children.

Can you say more about this? If we are speaking with children about trauma they have experienced, how can we do this without re-traumatising them?

When meeting with children about experiences of trauma, the story of this trauma and the effects that this has had on the child's life is often the first story that is brought to our attention. This story requires recognition.

But there is also a second story of how the child has responded to these experiences of trauma, and this second story is often overlooked. No-one is a passive recipient of trauma. Even children respond in ways to lessen the effects of the trauma, to seek comfort, to try to preserve what is precious to them, and so on. This second story is very important. The ways in which children respond to trauma are based on certain skills. These skills reflect what the child gives value to. And what the child gives value to is linked to the child's history, to their family, to their community, and to their culture.

These responses to trauma are not solely individual. They are not formed independently of the contribution of others. In these responses, children are linked to key figures of their lives. In narrative practice we are very interested in developing rich accounts of this second story. By developing rich accounts of this second story we reconnect children to culture, to family, to community, and to history.

How does this relate to considerations of creating 'safe' contexts for children to speak about their lives?

Often children are very reluctant to speak about the experiences of trauma that they have been through. There are many theories about this – that this is due to the child's denial, or that they have suppressed the trauma, and so on. But there is another explanation for this reluctance. If the child's identity has been defined by the trauma, and if there has not been any attention to second story development, then to invite children to speak about their experiences of trauma can be quite problematic. As I have already mentioned, it is quite hazardous to invite children to speak about their experiences of trauma if they don't yet have another place in which to stand. For children to speak about experiences of trauma in a single-storied way can reinforce the negative conclusions they have about their identity that were generated in the context of trauma. This can escalate their sense of shame. It can contribute to an increased sense of hopelessness, and it can be re-traumatising of the child.

I have heard you describe the importance of enabling children to have a 'different place to stand' prior to speaking about the trauma that they may have experienced. Can you say more about this?

Developing the second story is like developing a different territory of identity in which a child can stand and look out at their life, and reflect upon what they have been through. Once this different territory of life has been developed or redeveloped it becomes safe for a child to speak about the trauma they have been through.

I was recently teaching in Zimbabwe with a group of workers who respond to children who have been affected by HIV/AIDS. Within this group a metaphor was offered that beautifully describes this process. This metaphor was of assisting people to 'stand on the riverbank' in order to look at the river of life. According to the way this metaphor was employed, if one is floundering in the actual river in which the story of trauma dominates, and one is left struggling with the currents that are flowing past and around them, it is not possible to think differently about the events in which one has been immersed. But if one is standing in a different territory of identity, a territory that gives one a riverbank on which to stand, it is possible to look over the events of one's life, to re-visit them, to speak about them and to think differently about them, without being re-traumatised, without being swept along by the current.

What are some of the narrative practices that can assist in the development of a second story?

In the context of narrative practice we become vitally interested in the development of a second story in relation to traumatic experience. The rich development of a second story involves identifying the ways in which children have responded to the trauma they were subjected to, identifying how their responses are based upon what they give value to and what they hold precious, and tracing the history of what is valued and held precious, including how these are linked to the child's family, community, culture, and so on.

What does this rich development of the second story make possible?

Generating a rich description of the second story in this way provides options for children to re-engage with the first story, and to give expression to the experience of trauma without re-living the trauma, without being defined by the trauma.

It's important to note that developing this second story is not to undermine the significance of the trauma story. The story about trauma is not displaced. It is just that a second story develops alongside of it. These become parallel storylines. We begin to have double story conversations in which a second story unfolds in parallel with the trauma story.

The metaphor of a riverbank is a beautiful one ... it's not implying that the trauma story isn't significant, just that a child needs a different place to stand in relation to it ...

Yes. This second story provides a different territory of identity, like a riverbank, on which the child can stand when giving expression to their experiences of trauma. Standing on the riverbank makes it possible to look back and give voice to stories of trauma without being defined by the trauma. When standing on the riverbank it becomes possible to express experiences of trauma in ways that feature themes of outrage and reflections on injustice rather than as failure and shame. It is often the case that it only becomes possible for children, or for adults for that matter, to give a full account of what they have been through after they have another territory on which to stand. The second story provides a foundation for people to then give expression to experiences of trauma in ways that are healing and not re-traumatising. Furthermore, once the second story becomes richly described, it becomes a driving force for further healing actions. It becomes a driving force for people to take next steps that are in harmony with the understandings of what they give value to, and with what they intend for their lives, which are represented in this second story.

This seems a very different approach to responding to trauma than those notions which encourage children and adults to simply tell and re-tell the story of what they have been subjected to ...

These ideas about developing double-storied accounts of trauma provide a contrast to those associated with the modern notion of catharsis. This modern notion of catharsis is implicit in the idea that the pain of trauma is somehow 'held' within the body like a head of steam within a steam engine and that this needs to be 'discharged' in order for healing to take place. When this modern notion of catharsis influences counselling, people are sometimes invited to speak about only the experiences of the trauma they have been subject to. When the focus is directed only to the trauma, there is a potential for this to reinforce a single-storied sense of existence. This usually does not bring relief, and people often then feel compelled to find more and more avenues to 'discharge' and can end up feeling increasingly vulnerable and fragile.

You mentioned earlier that you pay particular attention to what children give value to in life. Can you say more about this?

When working with children who have been through trauma, we are interested in bringing forward the child's skills and what the child gives value to in life. We are then interested in tracing the social, relational, and cultural history of these skills and of what is given value, and of what has breathed life into these. If we can create contexts for children to speak about what is precious to them, they find themselves 'coming into life' in these conversations. It is, however, sometimes difficult to get onto what children value in life, because this is often hidden away in case it is further ridiculed or criticised. Narrative practitioners are on the look-out for any expressions of life, any statements that children make that provide a clue to their skills of living and to what they give value. This takes practice.

And once these are identified? What sort of exploration then takes place?

Once a counsellor hears the child say something that reflects the expression of a certain skill, or that might represent what the child holds precious, s/he can enquire into:

- What name the child would give to this skill, and/or to what is precious to them.
- The consequences of these skills and the consequences of holding onto something precious: How does this show up in their life? What does this bring to their life?
- How the child feels about this.
- What this all says about what's important to the child.
- The history of this in the child's life: who introduced the child to these skills, to what they hold precious, and to what they want for their lives;

who supported the development of these skills, how the child has sustained these over time, about how and when these first came to be important to the child; and so on.

These sorts of explorations open up space to identify threads or traces of a second story-line. Therapeutic conversations can then be used to thicken these threads into a meaningful second story. Building a second story of identity involves tracing a history, one in which there is a linking together of events in the child's life that are in harmony with the themes of these threads.

The rich development of this second story provides a foundation for an inquiry into children's traumatic experience. This is usually prompted by questions like: How did all of these things that we are learning about you help you to get through hard times? This sort of question positions children on the river bank as they begin to give an account of the trauma they have been subject to.

Experiences of trauma can be severely isolating. Are there ways in which this sense of isolation can be addressed?

Yes, and this is particularly significant in relation to traumatic experience that is associated with loss and grief. Again I'm reminded of the time I recently spent with workers in southern Africa who are responding to children who have lost to AIDS many of the adults in their families. In these circumstances, narrative practices can be engaged with to elevate the voices of the figures in children's lives who have been important to them. In this way, children's identities again become 'multi-voiced'. It is often possible to assist children to evoke the voices of parents and grandparents, even when they are no longer materially present. It is possible to bring these voices forward, and in this way children become less isolated and less bereft. It becomes possible for children to continue to experience the parents' wisdom with them in life.

What is the therapist's role in responding to children who are evoking the voices of those who have died ...?

For a person to bring forth the voices of lost loved ones is a skill. This skill has been eroded in white western culture but is still very present in many other cultures. The task for us is to find ways of validating and honouring this skill rather than disqualifying it. When a child demonstrates skills in bringing to the present their experience of their connection with their lost parents, siblings, grandparents, or other significant people in some way, we are able to inquire about:

- how they are able to do this,
- how this experience of evoking their lost loved one touches them,
- how they experience being nurtured through this,
- how they find personal warmth in this way.

In the context of HIV/AIDS in sub-Saharan Africa, I imagine this could be all the more relevant ...

Within epidemics like the HIV/AIDS epidemic, children can not only lose loved ones but also a sense of connection to culture, community, history and spirituality. Their sense of belonging can be lost. As an outcome of this, they can become non-social in their actions and this can have considerable consequences for their own lives and also the entire community. Finding ways to reconnect children to lost loved ones seems very important as this also enables a reconnection to a sense of community, history, culture and spirituality.

And re-membering conversations play a part in addressing this?

Re-membering conversations are a way of assisting children to bring forth the voices of lost loved ones. The 're-membering' metaphor is drawn from the work of Barbara Myerhoff who was a cultural anthropologist. To understand what is meant by re-membering conversations, it is first necessary to think about a person's life as a club with a membership. We can consider all those people with whom we are associated in the course of our lives as members of our 'club' of life. Some of these members we may have consciously invited into our lives, others we may have had little choice over including in our lives. In re-membering conversations, people deliberately choose who they would like to have more present as members of their club of life, and which memberships they would prefer to downgrade or revoke. The use of the term 're-membering' is therefore not just about passive recollection. One of the hopes of narrative practice is to contribute to a multi-voiced sense of identity, rather than a single-voiced sense of identity which is the outcome of loss, and that is often reinforced by some contemporary psychological practices. Re-membering conversations provide one avenue to the development of a multi-voiced sense of identity.

Am I right in thinking that there is another role for re-membering conversations ... that these are engaged with in order to thicken accounts of children's skills ...?

Yes. The skills of living that are so evident in these second stories of children's lives have been co-generated in the relationships with significant figures of their past. Re-membering conversations provide an opportunity for re-engaging with these significant figures. These figures do not necessarily have to be directly known in order to be identified as significant to a child's life. For example, these figures and identities may be the authors of books that have been important to the child, or characters in movies or comics. And these figures do not have to be people. For example, they may be the stuffed toys of a person's childhood, or a favourite pet, and so on. As we begin to hear stories about skills of living, it becomes possible to link the development of these skills to certain relationships from the child's past and present.

I have noticed that these re-membering conversations always emphasise the mutuality of these relationships. Is this significant?

Absolutely. One of the key aspects of re-membering conversations is that they generate two-way accounts of relationships. They create stories about relationships that emphasise the mutuality of these relationships, that emphasise the two-way exchange that is involved in these. In the first stage of re-membering conversations, the counsellor asks questions that seek stories about what the significant figure contributed to the child's life, and about what this suggests the figure appreciated about the child. But in the second stage of re-membering conversations, the counsellor asks questions that bring forth the second aspect of these relationships. These questions seek stories about the child's contribution to the life of the figure, and about how this was confirming of, or might have been confirming of, what life was all about for this figure.

Through these questions, children come to witness their identity through the eyes of the re-membered figure and give expression to how they might have touched this figure's sense of identity. This enables the child to draw new conclusions about their own worth and value.

Finally, it seems that when you are working with a child or children who have experienced trauma or loss, that much of your work involves trying to find ways to link the stories of their lives to the stories of others. Can you say more about this?

It is important to note that children's responses to trauma are not simply individual, independent responses. These responses have all been shaped by the relationships of history, by culture and by community traditions. One of the aims of narrative practice is to reconnect people with these relationships, and to culture and to community traditions. Bringing these connections alive, reinvigorating these connections, is a vital part of the therapeutic task. So much so that narrative practice is a bit like an introduction or re-introduction agency! This is not about counselling practice that is isolating of people. Rather, it is about exploring opportunities that might be available to people to experience their lives linked to others around certain valued themes.

Once a second story has been identified and has been redeveloped, it becomes important to find ways to further support this. There are a range of options that can contribute to the endurance of the second story, including practices of the written word.

Can you explain how you utilise practices of the written word when working with children?

When meeting with children about their experiences, it is usually possible to take some notes that document these conversations. These notes are always in the child's own words and can provide the basis of a therapeutic letter, a certificate of achievement, or the development of a story-book that can be read to the child each evening before going to sleep. These notes are often about particular skills and knowledges about life that the child has given expression to in our conversations with them, and these can be made more familiar to the child. These documents are usually highly treasured by children.

I have seen some of the certificates that are awarded to children in therapy contexts. Can you say something about these ...?

These certificates honour the efforts a child has made to respond to the circumstances that they have been faced with. For instance: 'This certificate hereby certifies that Megan has special abilities in caring for her brother and sisters through hard times. The ways that she has done this include: ....' These formal certificates are often placed in a highly visible position in the child's living space. This prompts care-givers, friends and visitors to ask questions about the certificate, thus encouraging the child to re-tell the story of how they handled the difficult circumstances in their lives.

What about therapeutic letters, how are these used?

These letters take many forms. For example, when working with children, a 'To whom it may concern' letter might be appropriate. This is a letter that the child can show to relatives, teachers, church members, and other members of the community, that describes the ways in which the child has responded to a range of circumstances and problems. This letter brings into focus the second story, and explicitly invites older young people and adults to respond in ways that are validating of this second story.

Apart from practices of the written word, are there other ways that can contribute to thickening a second story when working with children?

There are many other practices that contribute to the endurance of the second story. For instance, special community forums can be created in which adults are invited to 'a presentation evening'. Invitations are crafted and sent out to the significant people of the child's world, with details about why this special ceremony is taking place and about why the child is being awarded a particular certificate or other form of acknowledgement. There is a formal aspect to these ceremonies during which the child is presented with some sort of acknowledgement, such as a medal or some other trophy, or a certificate, which signifies their achievement in dealing with a particular difficulty. At these events it is usual for everyone present to play some part in a re-telling about why the child is receiving the award. After the formal part of the presentation there is a celebration which is usually lots of fun! These forms of community acknowledgement invariably make a significant difference in young people's lives.

Possibilities of this sort that contribute to the thickening of the second story when working with children are endless.

We started this conversation talking about considerations of trauma and now we're evoking ceremonies and fun! That seems an appropriate place to stop for now. Thanks Michael.

CHAPTER FOUR

Creating audiences for children's preferred stories

by Alice Morgan

In this paper I would like to share some of the ways that I have found to invite audiences to witness and become involved in the re-authoring of children's lives. Perhaps the best way to begin illustrating the potential of audiencing practices is by sharing Ebony's story.

Ebony (9 years)

One autumn morning soon after breakfast, I met with Ebony, Corey (Ebony's biological mother) and Ron (Ebony's step father). Corey had requested the appointment to discuss what she described as Ebony's 'tantrums' and 'appalling behaviour'. Corey also had some concerns about Ebony's eating patterns explaining that she often 'refused to eat or just eats tiny bits of food, she's really fussy'. Corey said she was at her wits' end with Ebony's behaviour as it was 'out of control' and she was concerned that Ebony was losing weight. Ron told me that he too thought Ebony was 'out of control', that he had tried everything he could think of, and that he had now 'run out of ideas'. He told me that he'd tried punishing Ebony, giving her rewards, ignoring her, buying her favourite foods, trying to make her feel special and withdrawing privileges like having her friends over to stay, all in an effort to help her. Ebony told me that 'school was getting harder' and that she thought 'life was not as fun as it used to be'.

In the early part of our meetings I asked a series of questions in order to assist Ebony, Corey and Ron to take a position in relation to the problem[1]. The name for the problem that the family agreed upon was 'the sad and worrying problem' that was making it hard for the family to enjoy their time together. They all said that they weren't happy about what it was doing to their lives and that they hoped for the 'closeness and fun' that they remembered to return as soon as possible. In these initial conversations I also heard more about the effects the problem was having on them, the worries it was causing and the conflict that they'd all noticed in their lives since the problem had snuck into their house about ten months previously. Whilst hearing about the problem and its effects, I was at the same time[2] beginning to notice some alternative descriptions of their relationships and lives. This enquiry opened the way for re-authoring conversations[3] that told stories about the things that were treasured in their family, what was important to them, and some of their hopes for the future. Importantly, I also came to hear about some of Ebony's personal qualities that everyone valued.

'She's always been so kind and caring of others', Corey offered. 'Yes, and creative. She's always loved to play and dance and sing and have fun. Other people are always telling us about her spark!' said Ron.

When I asked Ebony about what her parents were saying, she told me that she considered these personal qualities as 'good' and as something she thought 'did not fit' with the initial problem story. When I asked Ebony to describe how these qualities fitted with what she thought was important in life, she said: 'Well I want to make a better world for people'. This principle caught my attention and led me to ask many more questions. Through this enquiry about Ebony's values and commitments in life, we named some other things that Ebony valued about herself. I began to collect these descriptions as Ebony and her parents told me stories about the sorts of things Ebony valued:

'it's important to care for others and respect that everyone is not the same',

'enjoying a laugh',

'what matters is being close to people',

'doing something useful with my life'.

Having gathered many of these alternative descriptions and emerging preferred, alternative stories, I told the family that I'd be interested in finding out some more about them. Corey and Ron were the first audience I created for these preferred accounts of Ebony's identity to be witnessed and thickened. I interviewed Corey and Ron about their knowledge of Ebony in relation to these descriptions and asked them to tell me some stories that would fit with the qualities and commitments that Ebony had described.

Corey then told me some stories about when they were on holidays with another family and Ebony would always cuddle up to the other children and hug them when they were feeling sad, in order to make them happy again. Ron said he knew that Ebony enjoyed a laugh because she always chose funny movies to go to together. He told the story of a movie they had seen together about twelve months ago where 'Ebony and I were rolling around in the aisles it was so funny'. I heard many other stories about these preferred accounts of Ebony's life and identity. Ebony said she was really interested in these stories and that it made a positive difference to hear her mum and step-dad talk about them.

After hearing from Corey and Ron, I raised the idea of consulting other people who might have some stories about what Ebony valued in life. I was hoping to enlist the assistance of other outsider witnesses, other audiences. Ebony, Corey and Ron were enthusiastic about this idea so we set about writing a list of names of people who may have witnessed Ebony act in ways that would fit with the values we had been describing and who might be able to tell us some stories about these times. Ebony refined the list to people she was most interested in hearing from. Ron and Corey said they were sure that these people would 'do anything they could to help 'cos they've all been so worried about Ebony'. The people they identified were:

- Ebony's grade 2 teacher, Mr Decklin
- Ebony's aunt, Kath
- Ebony's best friend, Fiona
- The local shop owner, Mr Frances
- And Ebony's grandma, Beth, who lived in rural New South Wales

As it was not possible for all these people to come to my office, I suggested I could speak to them on the telephone instead. To arrange these phone conversations, we wrote a series of letters together explaining the reason for contacting each person and some of the things I'd be most interested hearing about. Ebony was keen to hand-deliver as many letters as possible and to personally address the letter to her grandma, who lived in another part of the country.

The following letter was sent to Kath, Mr Decklin, Mr Frances and Beth, and a modified version to Fiona, her school friend.

Dear

As you already know, I have been meeting with Ebony, Corey and Ron to help with some of the troubles that have come into their lives lately. They told me that you too have been worried about these troubles and might be willing to help out. So that is the reason for writing to you. I have heard some really interesting things about Ebony and what she stands for and I'm really curious to discover some more details about them.

Ebony has told me that:

- *'it's important to care for others and respect that everyone is not the same'*
- *she 'enjoys a laugh'*
- *'what matters is being close to people'*
- *she wants 'to do something useful with her life'*
- *she wants 'to make a better world for people'*

Ebony, Corey and Ron thought you may have some ideas or stories or knowledge of these that I could ask you about. Therefore I was wondering if we could arrange a short conversation over the telephone to ask you some questions? I would record our conversation and play it back to the family when we meet next.

I'd be most interested to discover anything you know about these commitments that Ebony holds for her life. For example[4]

- *Which of these commitments catch your attention?*
- *What images come to mind when you think of this commitment of Ebony's? Why do you think it struck a chord for you? What are you reminded of?*
- *What little stories can you think of that are evidence to you of these commitments?*

- *When have you witnessed or noticed these commitments in Ebony's life?*
- *How long ago did you notice these? What would you say they mean or seem to fit with?*
- *How has knowing that Ebony stands for these things contributed to your life?*
- *How has knowing Ebony's stories changed you? What might you do differently, as a result of knowing these stories for example? What has thinking of these stories reminded you of?*

I hope you are willing to help us out with this and look forward to talking with you.

Kind Regards,

Alice Morgan.

Over the course of the following weeks, I heard many wonderful stories from Kath, Mr Decklin, Fiona, Mr Frances and Beth. So much so that I could fill the pages of many books with their warmth and richness! Here are just a few of stories I heard.

Mr Decklin's reflections

Mr Decklin, Ebony's year 2 teacher, recounted times at school when he had witnessed Ebony's care and respect for others. On playground duty, for example, he said he would often (at least once a week) see Ebony talking to children who were lonely and including them in games. I asked him specific details about the many times he remembered when Ebony told jokes in class and made everyone laugh. He thought Ebony's interest in marine biology and recycling were examples of Ebony's commitments to care for the environment and to do something useful with her life.

In earlier conversations with Ebony, I had heard a little about her interest in being a marine biologist and how she thought it was important to 'care for the planet'. Mr Decklin's stories refreshed my memories of this and led me to be even more curious about them. Mr Decklin told me that he too was committed to ecology and that his connection with Ebony had supported him to decide to start an Environment Club at school. He told me that he always looked forward to seeing Ebony because of the laughs they shared and her funny sense of humour. This, he said, made it great to be a teacher: 'Knowing a kid like Ebony gives me hope that I can contribute to building a better world as well ... it keeps me motivated ... it makes my job seem worthwhile.'

Mr Frances' reflections

Mr Frances told me that he had witnessed Ebony's sense of humour at his shop. One day there was a young child, about three or four years old, who was crying and having a tantrum in his shop. Nobody knew what to do. Nothing seemed to be able to calm the child down, until Ebony arrived. Ebony started to pull funny faces and play 'peek-a-boo' with the child and within a few minutes, much to everyone's relief, laughter had replaced the screaming. Mr Frances thought that Ebony was a 'good kid', 'cos she was always polite to him, even though he didn't 'speak good English'. This, he said, he appreciated as it was something special that you don't always see and was evidence of Ebony's respect for people being different. Mr Frances said that knowing this about Ebony made him very happy. It made him think that 'Australia is a good country for my people to live in'.

Beth's reflections

On the day I spoke with Beth (Ebony's grandmother), Ebony and her family were in the room and we used the speaker phone so that everyone could hear the stories that Beth shared with me. Beth told me about how much she enjoyed Ebony coming for a sleepover at her house. She described the fun and mischief they got up to, like eating lollies at midnight, reading stories and watching videos together. Beth said that Ebony always chose videos or stories that were funny, and when they shared them together, Ebony liked to 'snuggle up' to her on the couch. Beth thought that these were signs that Ebony enjoyed a laugh and valued being close to people.

I had recorded the phone conversations that I shared with Kath, Mr Decklin, Fiona, Mr Frances and Beth, and each time I played these tapes back to Ebony, Corey and Ron I then asked the family some questions[5] about their experience of hearing the stories. In hearing these stories, what are you thinking about?

- What are your thoughts on what .... said?
- Do you remember the stories they spoke about?
- What is it like to hear about them?
- What is your opinion on what they said?
- Do you agree or disagree or see it a bit differently?
- What difference does it make to have heard what they said?

Over the weeks that these conversations took place, Corey described the process as 'life-changing'. She said that Ebony was 'coming back to her old self', and was 'getting her appetite back'. As time progressed, Corey said that Ebony 'was eating more the way she used to', that they were noticing her 'getting back into life' more: 'It's as though the more stories she heard, the easier things have been'. Ebony agreed with Corey saying: 'I never knew that people cared about those things. Hearing what people said made me want to do them more.' Ron described how Ebony was much happier in herself: 'We don't get the tantrums or anything now and she's joined the environment club at school. She got a certificate the other day.'

This certificate, it transpired, was something Ebony was very proud of. She had received it for 'friendliness to others and consistent effort'. As we admired the certificate together in my office, Ebony announced that she didn't think the family needed to come to therapy any more, and that instead they should come back one more time for a party 'to celebrate'. Ebony thought that if the troubles ever returned, all she needed to do would be to play the tapes of the stories I had gathered and 'that would fix it'.

The last time I saw Ebony and her family we had a party at the local playground. Fiona and Mr Decklin came along as well to help celebrate with chips, lemonade, lollies, sausage rolls and Ebony's favorite ice-cream cake. Ebony made sure we didn't leave any rubbish around when we left!

Creating Audiences

As the above story illustrates, creating audiences for children's preferred stories is an area of my work with children that brings an array of exciting possibilities. In my earlier years of practice with narrative ideas, engaging an audience was something that I would always try to do 'if there was time' or if it was 'convenient'. Reflecting back now, there were lots of opportunities that were missed.

As families and children have told me of the many positive ways that audiencing practices have contributed to their lives, I've also noticed the enormous difference an audience seems to make to the lives of people at the centre of the work. So much so that I now make sure that finding an audience is one thing that doesn't get missed. I now consider it one of my responsibilities as a therapist.

I can recall many joyful and memorable times which I have shared with people, animals, stuffed toys, through letter-writing, on the telephone, in parks, and over the internet as I've invited people to witness and become involved in the re-authoring of people's lives.

Identity as a social, relational and collaborative project[6]

Before giving some further examples of my work with children, I'd like to say a few things about identity and the thinking that informs the use of audiences in therapeutic contexts. There are many ways to understand the construction of identity, each with particular implications for therapeutic practice.

Nonstructuralist[7] ideas of the self view the self as constructed in relation to others, as a social and collaborative achievement. The formation of the self is understood as an ongoing process whereby the context and relationships of people's lives are significant and influential. In other words, identity is not formed in a vacuum nor is it innate, internal or unchanging over time. Identities are shaped by experiences and surroundings. They are socially constructed.

It is assumed therefore that, when children seek assistance for the predicaments of their lives, the view they hold of themselves and the stories they bring with them have been constructed and performed in relation to others. This construction of the self will affect what they do and the actions they take.

Just as problem stories are constructed in relation to others, so too can preferred accounts be witnessed and audienced[8] in relation to others. In narrative therapy we are interested in thickening the alternative and preferred identities of children's lives. Engaging audiences in a deliberate and particular way, known as outsider-witness practices, is one way to contribute to this. There are many purposes/intentions for engaging audiences in this work.

A narrative therapist is interested in the preferred stories of people's lives – the hidden, new or exceptional events of people's lives separate from the dominant, problem-saturated stories people usually bring to therapy. When preferred alternative stories are noticed and inquired about and audiences are engaged to witness them in a particular way[9], these preferred accounts of identity become more richly and thickly described.

Engaging audiences contributes to the revaluing of those things that people (in this case children) accord value, or hold dear and treasured. I have found in many cases that these treasured values, purposes in life, commitments or principles of living, are less visible or hidden: hidden under the weight of the dominant story; hidden because they have never before been thoroughly inquired about; hidden because their significance has been diminished by others; hidden or lost by the tricks and tactics of the problem. So, we are interested in opening space for the revaluing of those things that children give value to. One way to do this is by having witnesses to them.

Engaging these audiences cannot, however, be left to chance. The revaluing of children's treasured values by an audience does not happen without the therapist structuring the conversation in a particular way. The questions I asked Mr Decklin, Beth, Mr Frances, Kath and Fiona, were chosen specifically to invite them to speak in ways that would resonate for Ebony. My role was to establish a context in which the things that were important to Ebony could reverberate or resonate with the lives of the witnesses.

There were particular steps I took to ensure that the retelling by the audience members resonated for Ebony. In this definitional ceremony, I used outsider-witness questions that would;

1) Identify the expression
   e.g. What caught your attention? What struck a chord for you?
2) Describe the image that was evoked for the person
   e.g. What did this have you thinking about in your own life?
3) Embody the response
   e.g. What is it about your own life that accounts for why these images caught your attention?
4) Acknowledge transport
   e.g. How has knowing Ebony's stories changed you? As a result of knowing these stories, what might you do differently? What has thinking of these stories reminded you of?

These types of questions invited all those people chosen by Ebony to be witnesses, to say things so as to evoke images that would link with images in her own life. In the evoking of these images, like sound waves, they bounced out from her, touched on the themes or images in Mr Decklin's stories and ricocheted back to Ebony. As this 'bouncing' or reverberation was experienced by those present, the images or shapes of the preferred stories of Ebony's life became more visible and clearly defined.

When people, in this case children, experience resonance, it also contributes to a sense of their lives being linked with the lives of others around similar themes; their values or commitments are echoed with the values and commitments of others. Through conversations with Mr Decklin, for example, we heard how Ebony and he shared a similar commitment to caring for the environment. Ebony and Ron both valued 'having a laugh', and Ebony and Beth were joined around their values of being close to people. Asking questions in these ways moves away from ideas about, for example: finding things that people have in common toward intentionally building resonant images of Ebony's preferred self.

I think of resonance as being a bit like sound waves emanating from a central point and bouncing back and forth as they touch on other objects. Each time they bounce or touch something else they grow stronger or are more easily heard or recognised. The questions I asked intended to enable the themes and commitments held precious by Ebony to touch the lives of others (e.g. Mr Decklin). As they touched the lives of others and bounced back to Ebony, her treasured values became even clearer and more visible. Through this process, it is as though people become more 'on the same wave length'. Each time these images are bounced back and forth, the image becomes clearer, visible and more defined.

When people experience the type of resonant response described in this paper, they have often told me how valuable they have found it. They say that these sorts of responses contribute to a sense that their lives are 'not for nothing', and that instead their lives have a significant purpose. This, they have told me, has been very important to them in addressing the predicament for which they first sought help.

The examples in this paper hope to show how the therapy was structured to ensure that the children at the centre of the meetings experienced a resonance of the values and commitments in their lives, with the lives of others. The children and families consulting me, through these audiences, heard the ways in which their story bounced off and connected with the lives of others, making this preferred story clearer and more visible.

When this is achieved, the preferred stories for the children and families' lives and relationships become more thickly described and, in turn, their actions are then shaped more in accordance with them. In this way, spaces are created for children to do things that fit with these preferred stories. When children act in accordance with these preferred accounts of who they are and what is important to them, in connection with other people's values and commitments, they have managed to renegotiate their relationship with the problem they initially sought help for and, in so doing, usually no longer need our assistance[10].

Some background to the stories

Before sharing some further stories of the ways I have found to engage audiences in preferred accounts of children's lives, there are some general things I wish to say. Firstly, all the children mentioned in this paper were in a safe context whilst I was meeting with them, and any abuse that may have occurred in the past was no longer present. Secondly, the stories included in this paper are not entire nor full accounts of the therapy. In order to stay within the realms of this paper, I have only explained the parts of our meetings that involved audiences or witnesses. Before audiencing practices were engaged in, a number of other practices of narrative therapy were explored. For instance, earlier therapy sessions had created space for the child and family to articulate their position in relation to the problem by using the Statement of Position Map[11], and we had engaged in many re-authoring conversations[12] together. These re-authoring conversations in which preferred accounts of identity begin to be co-authored, lay the foundation that is required before witnesses are engaged. The preferred stories of identity that are described through re-authoring conversations are then thickened and more richly described through inviting audiences and witnesses.

In the examples I have included below, I have tried to write about what happened with some sense of the order in which the events occurred. In doing so, there may appear to be a smooth and progressive sequence of questions, responses and events. This is because I am yet to acquire the skill which children display in being able to flip and change, weave in and out of an array of things all happening at once. If I was to acquire this skill, the writing of these stories would more reflect the array of things that happened all at once each time I met with the children concerned. Until then, here are two more stories about creating audiences for children's preferred stories.

Toby (6 years)

Toby's mother, Michele, requested an appointment to see about 'Toby's diagnosis of ADD'. At our first meeting she explained how, since the diagnosis and medication, Toby was 'a little bit better' but she thought there 'should be more we can do for him'. 'I want to be sure I've done all I can for him', she explained. She thought that Toby would be interested in meeting me so we arranged a time when we could meet together.

One week later an energetic, friendly and inquisitive boy bounded into my office, curious to explore all the toys, stuffed animals, pictures and books in the room. He had many questions to ask me before I was allowed to ask him what was important to talk about. 'My ADV' he told me. Michele quickly corrected him saying 'No Toby, it is ADD. That's what makes you go silly.'

In these early meetings we exposed 'Jimmy Jumpy'[13] and all the things it got up to in Toby's life. Through drawing pictures, playing with the stuffed toys and asking questions, we found out a lot about what 'Jimmy Jumpy' did and what Toby thought about it. Toby was sure that 'Jimmy Jumpy' was 'bad news' in his life and 'was a badie like Voltemarte (from Harry Potter movie)'. Through this externalising conversation, I began to hear about some of the differences between what Jimmy Jumpy stood for and what Toby stood for in life. For instance, I heard how 'Jimmy Jumpy' liked to hop around during movies but Toby liked to 'watch the whole thing'. How Jimmy Jumpy was 'out for trouble' but Toby was 'out for being friendly and having friends'. How Jimmy Jumpy liked to 'create mess and get people shouting' and about how Toby 'liked his room to be a bit tidy so he could find his toys'.

By this time, Toby had formed a close relationship with Herme, a small brown bear, and Abergaile, a somewhat scruffy pink bear, who both occupied a chair in my room. Toby offered to care for Herme and Abergaile and to take them home to introduce them to his bear, Boris. Herme, I explained, loved visiting other houses and was a bit of a detective. Toby liked this idea and asked me what I meant by detective. I explained that Herme discovered things about people: about what people are good at, about how they like to live their lives, about how they stick to what's important to them.

I explained that Abergaile liked to help children too and I wondered what help Toby might need from Abergaile.

Toby said: 'She can be the spotter'.

'The Spotter?' I asked as it was an unfamiliar term to me[14].

'Yes, spotting out for Jimmy Jumpy.'

'And when she's spotted Jimmy Jumpy, what should she do?' I asked.

'Yell at me and I'll do something about it' he replied.

So that is what happened. Herme and Abergaile went to visit Toby as the Detective and the Spotter. At our future meetings with Toby and Michele, Herme and Abergaile became the perfect audience for me to ask questions of in relation to Toby's skills, preferences, values and hopes. At future meetings I interviewed the toys, with Toby speaking on their behalf. These conversations evoked stories that thickened alternative accounts of Toby's identity, accounts that distinguished what he stood for compared to what Jimmy Jumpy was up to.

As these alternative accounts of Toby's life were witnessed by Herme and Abergaile, many other opportunities for engaging audiences emerged. On one occasion, for example, Herme told me that Toby had been chosen to be 'the leader' at school. This, Herme explained, meant that Toby was 'growing up and meant that he wanted to do better at school'. I asked Herme if she knew of anyone else who would know something about this? Anyone who might have witnessed this?' Herme thought for a while and suggested that Colin, Toby's swimming coach, might know.

Michele suggested that Colin was very quick at emails, so I quickly wrote to him (with Toby and Michele's permission) seeking more stories that supported Toby's wishes to 'be better at school'. Colin described some other times when he had seen this working for Toby. Through my questions (similar to the one in the previous letter). Colin told me that he too had wanted 'something better for Toby at school' and thought it was very 'encouraging' to know what Toby was doing.

One day, out of the blue, I received an email from Toby's school teacher, Mrs Marshall, who wanted to tell me a bit about what she was noticing about Toby at school. It turned out that Michele had suggested Mrs Marshall email me with some of the things she had told Michele about Toby's recent actions. Mrs Marshall wrote with some examples of times she had witnessed Toby 'doing a great job'. I exchanged a few notes with Mrs Marshall (with me asking her a few questions and Mrs Marshall answering), and I shared these notes with Toby and Michele at our meetings. Michele told me that Toby 'couldn't wait' to get to our meetings so that he could hear more stories from the people and stuffed animals I was talking to about Toby's achievements.

As more and more stories were told and witnessed, Jimmy Jumpy started to, as Abergaile described it, 'get the message that he wasn't needed as much'. Just as Jimmy Jumpy wasn't needed so much, neither was I! So, to conclude the series of meetings, I prepared a statement (in the form of a certificate) that outlined all the things we had discovered about Toby: what he was on about; what he thought was important; what he was good at; what he wanted his life to be like. Each witness that had been involved was invited to sign the statement and write a sentence or two in support of it. They were only too happy to oblige with this.

As far as I know, Herme and Abergaile still enjoy living at Toby's house and the cerificate takes pride of place on the back of the pantry door at his house. Toby continues with the medication prescribed and Jimmy Jumpy is back 'where Toby wants him'. That is, 'it comes back to visit every now and again but Toby doesn't let him cause as much trouble as it used to'.

The examples I have discussed so far have illustrated how I have engaged audiences with children in therapeutic contexts with other family members, with children's supportive friends and imaginary toys. The final example tells the story of some ways I engaged audiences with children in a group context.

In Group contexts

Amanda, Colin, Tony, Beth and Aiden (between 7 and 9 years of age) were meeting with me about what their teachers described as 'low self-esteem'. Our conversations focused around some of the important things to them in their lives. Through re-authoring conversations, each child made a book containing a story about them and their lives. I helped the children draft and redraft their story using the computer, and each child dictated the words they wanted recorded. Sometimes I would ask: 'What do you think that says about what sort of a world you want to be part of?' or questions to help with the structure of the story, e.g.: 'What came next?' or questions that included the voices of supportive people in the child's life: 'Why wasn't your mum surprised that you could do that? What does she know about you that would tell her you were on about that?'

The children's colourful illustrations and artwork decorated these magnificent books that each child treasured. When they were complete, there were many opportunities for audiences to be engaged to witness them.

The first audience were the members of the group themselves. During the subsequent times we met, the children read their particular story to the other members of the group. Then I provided them a 'worksheet' with some sentences for them to finish.

Sentence starters:

The thing that stood out to me the most was ....

The picture that came to me was ....

I imagined..

It stood out to me because..

Now I know Colin's story I will ....

Or Now I know Colin's story I might ....

Or It has taken me to ....
(How has hearing this story changed you? Where has it taken you that you might not otherwise have gone?)

Those children who were able to write, completed the sentences themselves and I was available to scribe for others and scaffold[15] other questions so they could respond. Some children preferred to draw their reflection instead of writing, using the sentence starters as a prompt for their illustrations. These pages were then photocopied (so every child had a copy) and the original was stapled at the back of the child's book (i.e. the child whose story was being witnessed, in this case Colin).

After the pages were complete and collated, I interviewed the children about what this process was like for them. Many said that they liked what people had drawn for them and that they liked learning what the other children thought of them. Some of their comments included: 'I didn't know that he thinks the same way as me', and: 'It makes me happy'.

Many more audiences were then engaged. When the children returned to their classrooms, their teachers offered them the opportunity to read their story to their classmates. All of the children 'jumped at the chance'. The teachers used the sentence starters to ask the classmates their response to the story they heard. One at a time, the child at the centre heard how their story touched the lives of the other children in their classroom. One teacher told me she felt quite overwhelmed, at first with the story and then with the responses of the other children: 'It was so supportive of her. It painted her in a different light and the children can now see her in a more positive way.' Another teacher placed some 'congratulatory' stickers on the back cover of Amanda's book. Later on, she proudly showed these stickers, pictures and book at a school assembly.

Having heard Aiden's story, one class was so interested in the idea that they spent several of the next few weeks drafting and redrafting their own stories. Each child read their story to the class and children responded to what they heard. Aiden became the 'expert' and a 'consultant' in this process. Aiden's mother told me that 'he now comes home glowing from school. Just having the other children asking him what to do next or checking something with him, gives him a sense that he has something to offer.'

Each time the stories were shared at home with parents, aunties, uncles, grandparents, carers, nextdoor neighbours, godparents, babysitters, special friends, at Sunday School, at Greek School and at bedtime, a further audience was created. The sentence starters prompted people to respond to the story in a particular way that built resonance for the child at the centre. Their responses contributed to the further rich description of these stories by acknowledging how one person's life is linked with the lives of others around shared themes, principles, values or dreams. As these books are kept and treasured over the coming years, I wonder just how many more people will be invited to act as witnesses?

Conclusion

The stories I have shared about the ways in which I have engaged audiences to preferred stories in children's lives are only a few. I hope they might encourage others to try out these practices more, to make time to do them, to take up this responsibility in their work. I hold many fond memories of the contribution these practices have made to my work in encouraging me and in sustaining my enthusiasm and hope. My warmest wishes with your discoveries.

Notes

1. These questions were centred around the Statement of Position Map. See Chapter 1 of this book or Morgan (2000).
2. This double listening involves attention to the absent but implicit. See White (2000, chapter 3).
3. See Carey & Russell (2004, chapter 2).
4. The categories of inquiry in this letter are informed by Michael White's categories of outsider witness response (White 2004b). For more information about outsider witness responses see also Carey & Russell (2004, chapter 4).
5. See Carey & Russell (2004, chapter 4); White (2004a); Morgan (2000, chapter 14).
6. See White (2004, chapters 3 and 4).
7. Non-structuralist enquiries therefore become fascinated with the particularities of people's lives, their actions that are an expression of certain intentions, commitments, principles, hopes, dreams, passions, beliefs and values rather than one's motives, strengths, deficits, drives, characteristics, talents, personality traits, resources or needs. See White (2004, chapter 3).
8. When working with children, the power differences between adults and children are an important consideration when thinking about how adults can affect the stories children have about their life and relationships. See also Chapter 2 of this book.
9. These practices are referred to as outsider witness groups and definitional ceremony. See also Carey & Russel (2004, chapter 4); White (2004b).
10. See White (2004b).
11. See Chapter 1 of this book and Morgan (2000, pp.17-44).
12. See Carey & Russel (2004, chapter 2); Morgan (2000, chapter 8).
13. These practices are known as personification of the problem. See Chapter 1 of this book and Morgan (2000, chapter 3).
14. I later discovered that this was a term used in a popular playground game similar to hide-and-seek for the person who stood at home base and tried to watch out for people trying to reach it.
15. See Chapter 1 of this book for more about scaffolding questions.

References

Carey, M. & Russell, S. 2004: *Narrative Therapy: Responding to your questions.* Adelaide: Dulwich Centre Publications.

Morgan, A. 2000: *What is Narrative Therapy? An easy-to-read introduction.* Adelaide: Dulwich Centre Publications.

White, M. 2000: *Reflections on Narrative Practice; Essays and interviews.* Adelaide: Dulwich Centre Publications.

White, M. 2004a: *Narrative Practice and Exotic Lives; Resurrecting diversity in everyday life.* Adelaide: Dulwich Centre Publications.

White, M. 2004b: 'Working with people who are suffering the consequences of multiple trauma: A narrative perspective.' *International Journal of Narrative Therapy and Community Work, No.1.*

CHAPTER FIVE

Fostering collaboration - between parents and children, and between child protection services and families

an interview with Michael White

I imagine most therapists can recall times in their practice when meetings with children/young people and their parents have been filled with expressions of conflict and misunderstanding. Would you be happy to speak about what you try to keep in mind as a therapist in these moments?

I often meet with families where there is conflict between children or adolescents and their parents. This conflict has usually contributed to many misunderstandings, hurt feelings, and negative conclusions about the motives of the other. At times this conflict has escalated to the point that there is a near total breakdown of collaboration between these parties, who have become quite polarised. Families often seek the assistance of therapists at this time. In these circumstances, I am very interested in developing avenues for conversation that can foster collaboration.

When families with children and adolescents seek consultation, very often the problem has been collapsed onto the lives of these young people. In the eyes of the parents, and very often in the eyes of the young person, the problem has become a reflection of the young person's identity. As an outcome of this, parents and young people can be quite conflicted with each other over the problem. In these circumstances, externalised definitions of the problem can be negotiated that open space for a broadening of the conversation (see chapter 1 in this book).

In the context of an externalising conversation, it can be very helpful to these parents and children to have an opportunity to identify a broad range of consequences of the problem in their lives and in their relationships with each other. In identifying these consequences, parents, as well as young people, have the opportunity to give expression to their experience of their frustrations and disappointments in ways that can significantly diminish the conflict over the problem.

Can you say more about why it's so important for parents, as well as children, to have a chance to speak about the effects that the particular difficulties or conflict is having on their lives?

When people find themselves in conflict that is longstanding, and when people are responding to the longstanding conflicts of others, they are often tempted to totalise one party. When it comes to family conflict it can be children or parents who are totalised. Within families it is more often that children are totalised. Within the culture of psychotherapy it is more often the parents who are totalised, and most commonly the mother. The outcome of this is invariably negative. Usually the child and the parents become more alienated from each other as a result of this, and parents become alienated from the counsellor. In initial externalising conversations, it's very important that the influence of the problem on the lives of the parents is not overlooked. Parents can be highly frustrated and anxious about problems they have experienced with their children, and in this context it can be difficult for them to listen to their children's account of the problem and its effects on their own lives.

Can you say more about how these conversations unfold? It is so easy in these circumstances for conversations to descend into parental complaint and then children's denial and then further complaint, and so on ... how can this be avoided?

I am very aware of the responsibility that I have to provide an opportunity for these conversations to go well. There are lots of ways of observing this responsibility. If parents are expressing complaints or criticism in relation to some aspect of their daughter or son's life, one option is to interview them about the absent but implicit that is expressed in these complaints. I might inquire as to what these complaints represent in terms of the concerns that the parents have about aspects of their daughter or son's life, in terms of concerns relating to their own lives, and in terms of their relationships with their son or daughter. These concerns might be linked to certain hopes that seem threatened, to values that are being compromised, to purposes that are being frustrated, to aspirations that are being eroded, to a respect for oneself that is being undermined, and so on.

Talking about concerns, and the foundation of these concerns, as well as complaints, enables different sorts of conversations to unfold. For instance, it becomes possible to ask questions that trace a history of what these concerns are founded on. In these circumstances, parents will have an opportunity to speak about particular experiences within their history that are implicated in the development of these hopes, purposes and values. In this way, the initial criticisms and complaints become more particular and more personal as they are embodied in the parents' experiences. As these criticisms and complaints become more particular and personal in this way, the son or daughter is relieved of some of the negative conclusions that have been constructed about their identity. This also has the effect of opening space for the daughter or son to speak of their own concerns, and of the foundation of these concerns.

When this has been achieved, it is then possible to interview the son or daughter about whether they share any of these concerns that the parents have for them, for their own lives, and for their relationship with their son or daughter. At this time it is usually the case that at least one concern of all those expressed is identified as a shared concern. If any of the parents' concerns are even minimally confirmed by the son or daughter, there is now a degree of shared understanding that can provide a foundation for collaborative inquiry. It becomes possible for family members to talk more about not just this shared concern but also about what it is linked to in a way in which all of this becomes much more richly understood. This invariably provides a platform for collaborative action to address the concern.

But what if the child does not share any of the parents' concerns?

If the son or daughter does not share any of the parents' concerns, this provides an opportunity to ask him or her more about this. S/he can be interviewed about why s/he does not have these concerns about their own life, or about their parents' lives, or about their relationships with their parents.

The son or daughter's response to this inquiry can be taken up into a conversation in which they have an opportunity not only to distinguish their own concerns from the concerns of their parents, but to also give an account of the sort of knowledges of life and skills of living that they are developing that provide them with an assurance they needn't be troubled about the concerns that their parents have for their lives. Action that is being taken by the daughter or son on the basis of these knowledges and skills can then be explored.

I find that when these young people have the opportunity to describe their own concerns, as well as the foundation of these concerns in terms of their own hopes, values, purposes, aspirations, and so on, and when they have the opportunity to give an account of their knowledges of life and skills of living that provide them with some assurance that they needn't be troubled by the concerns that their parents have for their lives, that this mitigates their parents' concerns. Not only do parents get some sense that their son or daughter does have their hand on the rudder in guiding their own life, but that their son or daughter also possesses some knowledges and skills that are available to them in the management of the predicaments of their life.

Another benefit of this inquiry is that young people have the opportunity to more richly describe what they give value to and what they intend for their lives, as well as these knowledges and skills, and this becomes more available to them and influential in the shaping of their own actions.

Alternatively, the daughter or son can be interviewed about their understandings of the effects of their parents' concerns on their relationships with their parents and the consequences of this on their own lives. Questions can be asked about which aspects of these consequences they consider unsatisfactory, about why they consider these consequences unsatisfactory, and about what options are available to them that might diminish or resolve these concerns of the parents. This inquiry can open space for young people to speak of what they give value to and of what they intend for their lives, and of the skills available to them in shaping their relationships with others.

I can imagine that it's important to have these different options in mind as you undertake these conversations!

Yes. It's important to know that, whichever way the conversation turns, there are possible avenues to explore that will contribute to fostering collaboration between family members and between the therapist and the family.

What about circumstances in which young people have complaints about their parents?

In this conversation we've mostly been focusing on complaints and concerns that parents have about their children. But young people also have complaints and concerns about their parents and it is possible to address these by inverting the approach that I've been discussing here.

Are there other particular ways in which collaboration can be fostered in conversations with families with children?

There are many. Perhaps I can mention just one other here. This involves positively implicating parents in the skills and knowledge displayed by their children, and is particularly relevant when parents are feeling inadequate and are seeing themselves as failures in their parental roles.

There is a tradition within the field of psychotherapy of negatively implicating parents in children's lives. In other words, whenever a child displays some action that is deemed undesirable, the parent or care-givers are routinely seen to be implicated in this. This tradition of negatively implicating parents often has negative effects for both parents and children. It can have the effect of dividing the child from the parents, reinforcing a sense of incompetency for parents, and it makes it more difficult for the child to be on reasonable terms with their own history.

As an antidote to this, there are many ways in which parents can be implicated positively in their children's expressions of skills and knowledge of life. This is possible even when there are aspects of the parents' management of child-rearing responsibilities that are potentially or actually traumatising. Of course, if a child is being traumatised by their parents, this must be acknowledged and addressed. This is always given priority. However, efforts to address these potentially or actually negative aspects of the parents' actions can be facilitated through implicating the parents positively in aspects of their children's expressions of life.

Can you say more about this?

In the course of therapeutic conversations, it is possible to identify initiatives of the daughter or son that are expressions of competence. These might be initiatives that are demonstrated during the conversation, or they might be initiatives of recent history, for example in stories of the child's actions that demonstrate particular skills and knowledge. These initiatives can be rendered more significant in therapeutic conversations, and the particular knowledges of life and skills of living that the child has demonstrated can be drawn out.

Having accomplished this, a therapeutic inquiry can then bring significant focus to the parents' contribution to the development of these knowledges of life and skills of living expressed in the daughter or son's initiative. This can be done in a way that doesn't subtract in any way from the child's accomplishment.

Are you saying that, in exploring the social and relational history of children's skills and knowledge, it is often the case that parents are implicated in the development of these skills and knowledge?

Yes. It is possible to engage in conversations that implicate parents positively in relation to their children's development of certain skills and knowledges. By tracing the history of a child's knowledge and skills, the relational, social and cultural richness of their life becomes more visible. This provides new options for the child to be on reasonable terms with their own history and provides for the development of a stronger sense of self. And being implicated in the development of some of the special skills and knowledges expressed by their children provides these parents with a place to stand from which they are able to review and to critique aspects of their care-taking that might contribute to undesirable outcomes for their children and for their relationships with them. This positive implication can free parents from a totalisation of their identity in terms of what has gone wrong in their relationships with their children, which releases them from a 'defended posture'.

I would be very interested to hear about whether you think these sorts of collaborative practices are relevant within child protection investigations, in which workers are trying to respond to possible acts of abuse or neglect ...

This is a big topic! The history of child protection action is not a history of collaboration between state agencies and the families being investigated. When speaking with those who have been principally involved in child protection action, when the circumstances are right and people feel that they can be frank, it is very common to hear expressions of regret, regret about how various situations were managed. This regret is not only expressed in relation to the child protection events of decades past, but also in relation to events of more recent history, of contemporary times. In these conversations, regrets are often expressed by people who have worked in child protection investigation, by those responsible for the formulation of child protection policy, and by those people who have been subject to child protection investigation and action, including most parents and a great many of those young people who have been the focus of such investigation and action.

It is an area that is often seen to be pretty fraught with complexities. Are there ways in which child protection responses could be more collaborative?

In recent times there has been a growing society-wide awareness of the negative consequences of non-collaborative child protection action, of child protection action that is not founded upon collaboration between child protection services and the families that are the subject of child protection investigation. On account of this, there have been a number of developments relating to more collaborative approaches to child protection investigation. For example, state agencies in various places have instituted programs for meetings with the families of children who are the focus of child protection investigations with the objective of encouraging parents, and at times siblings, to formulate plans that would ensure the safety of the child. In many instances, these meetings occur prior to the institution of more formal legal procedures, and the intention is for the outcome of these meetings to shape any decisions that are made down the track.

These and other initiatives in more collaborative approaches to child protection investigation and action are significant. However, this is only a beginning, and there is still much to be done. For example, now that these forums for consulting families about the safety of children have been developed, what do we need to put into place so that families are prepared to step into these forums with a voice on matters like safety, and with a voice on options for actions that might not just preserve safety and ensure responsibility, but that also might provide some foundation for the recovery of their relationships with the children who are the focus of child protection investigation, and for the redevelopment of these relationships in which the life-giving aspects of these are elevated?

This is an important question because, in many of these families, the very notion of safety is not a generalised concept, and it is important that there be the opportunity for these families to develop this concept ahead of stepping into these forums that are part of the institutionalisation of collaboration in child protection action and investigation. The same can be said about the concept of responsibility. This is often a very underdeveloped concept, particularly for those parents who perpetrate abuse. This is the case for the concept of responsibility for actions that are abusive or neglectful, for the concept of responsibility for ensuring security and safety for the child, and for the concept of responsibility for actions that might be healing for the child. The further development of these concepts of responsibility is a factor quite critical to the parents' participation in these forums, to them having a voice on safety issues, and to them having a voice on life-giving options in regard to child protection action. This focus on concept development brings to our attention the importance of adequate preparation for parents' participation in these forums that have been instituted to promote collaboration.

There is much to be done in developing approaches to child protection that are more fully collaborative, in developing approaches that will be effective in addressing the regret that is expressed across the decades of child-protection investigation and action. I believe that the development of these approaches will significantly reduce the potential for regret in the future.

What are some other areas within child protection investigations that could be carried out with a greater sense of collaboration?

There are many of these. I have talked about the critical importance of the development of concepts of responsibility. However, at this present time, in most places, legal processes linked to child protection action are not favourable to this development. In fact, it is usually the case that courts are discouraging of this. In the context of law courts, those who acknowledge responsibility for actions that are abusive or neglectful are punished, and this often includes incarceration. Those who deny this responsibility usually suffer few if any consequences before the law. So there is much rethinking to be done about this aspect of child protection investigation, and I believe that this predicament could be effectively addressed in the context of more truly collaborative partnerships between the courts and child protection agencies.

One of the areas in which there is scope for more collaboration in child protection investigation and action is in the consultation of children, and about the lives of children, who are the focus of these investigations. Usually this consultation is shaped by an agenda to determine the facts of the alleged abuse or neglect that these children have been subject to, to identify the consequences of this abuse and/or neglect and, on occasions, to then provide an opportunity for these children to express their experiences of this abuse and/or neglect in ways that might be healing. Rarely, in my experience, is there a significant focus on investigating the actual responses made by these children to what is perceived to be abusive and/or neglectful.

Do you have any idea as to why these sorts of extended consultations of children are so rare?

There are many normative ideas about childhood, and some of these pose an impediment to the extended consultation of these children in child protection investigation. The evaluation of young people's lives against these normative ideas, many of which are founded upon developmental theories, particularly comes into play when the child's role in the family transgresses a taken-for-granted relationship arrangement; when aspects of the child's role conflict with routine and accepted assumptions about the nature of parent/child and child/sibling relationships. Often it is the young person's performance of aspects of the roles that are assumed to be the usual responsibility and sole province of parenthood that triggers this evaluation. These evaluations are frequently expressed in pathologising diagnoses like: 'This is a parentified child', or in negative and popular conclusions like: 'This child is being robbed of his/her childhood'. Such evaluations are usually associated with the forecast of dire consequences, like: 'The outcome of this will be a condition of arrested development in this child'.

I've met many children who are considered 'parentified' and on every occasion it has been clearly apparent that these children are skilled in the nurturing, care-taking and supervision of others. It has always been possible to play a part in acknowledging and honouring these skills, and for children to take pride in their development of these. And it has also been possible to establish support for these children in the expression of these skills, and by providing them with periods of respite. I have also met many adults who, as children, played parental roles in their families, and who were judged to have arrested development on account of this. These adults have lamented aspects of this role in their childhood, but have also acknowledged the possibilities brought to their lives by the care-taking competencies that were established in their childhood. And few, if any, of these people experienced any acknowledgement of these competencies in childhood, or were supported in their parental role. Just imagine the difference that it makes for children to experience acknowledgement for this in childhood!

What implications does this have in thinking about child protection?

When a primary basis for child protection action is theoretical, as in the case of developmental theory providing the foundation for norms against which the child's life is being measured, it becomes very difficult to engage in the sort of extended consultation of young people, and of the parents and siblings, that will provide an account of the actual responses of these young people to the abuses and or/neglect that they are perceived to be subject to. I don't want to be misunderstood on this, for I am not suggesting that developmental theory is irrelevant, or that children's minds are simply more compact versions of the minds of adults; that a child's consciousness is a mini version of adult consciousness. I will reiterate: to take developmental theory and the norms that it sponsors as a primary basis for the evaluation of the young person in response to concerns about the consequences of what is perceived to be abusive and neglectful, is an impediment to the extended consultation of young people, and of their parents and siblings, about the responses of these young people to this perceived abuse and neglect.

On occasions I have also heard you speak about how you think ideas of eugenics continue to influence child protection work. Can you say something about this here?

Yes, I think this is relevant. It is not only norms sponsored by developmental theory that are an impediment to the extended consultation of young people. There are also norms inspired by a modern-day eugenics agenda.

This implicit eugenics agenda is present in conclusions like: 'This child would be better off in a more normal family'. The evaluation of young people's lives according to the norms inspired by this eugenics agenda is often triggered by the presence of disability in one or both of the young person's parents, but is not restricted to this. Historically, eugenics was a movement that was initiated in England in the late nineteenth century. It was a pseudo-scientific movement that sponsored programs for breeding out the characteristics of human life that were considered undesirable. The eugenics movement reached the pinnacle of its achievement mid-twentieth century, and from then on went into a state of decline, being thoroughly discredited in the later decades of the twentieth century. However, I believe that the shadow of this movement and the sentiments about life associated with it, can still be quite influential in shaping the assessment of the needs of young people who are the focus of child protection investigation and action.

What implications does this have for practitioners?

I think it's important to make visible the impediments to the extended consultation of young people. This includes those practices of evaluation of young people's lives against norms that are sponsored by developmental theory and those that are inspired by an implicit eugenics agenda. These are not the only impediments to this extended consultation, but they seem to me to be high up on the list. Rendering these impediments visible has the effect of opening new avenues of inquiry about young people's experience of what is perceived to be abusive and neglectful. Some of these avenues of inquiry provide rich accounts of young people's responses to their experiences of abuse and neglect.

Why is it significant to inquire about children's responses to their experiences of abuse and neglect?

Although it is invariably the case that children do respond to the traumas they are subject to, rarely do I find that they are familiar with these. In fact, at the outset of my conversations with people who consult me about the consequences of trauma in their lives, it is usually the case that their response to what they were subject to is not available to conscious recall. One outcome of this is that children are constructed as passive recipients of the traumas they have been subject to, and this has a highly negative effect on the development of their sense of personal agency – on the development of a sense of being able to intervene in the shaping of their existence, of a sense of the world being responsive to the fact of their existence. Needless to say, this is highly disabling! It contributes to feelings of impotence, emotional paralysis, of futility, and of personal desolation. Very often, due to the limited nature of inquiry in professional contexts, this can eventuate in a lifestyle that has been characterised as one of 'learned helplessness'.

What is an alternative? When working with children who have experienced significant trauma, how can we orientate ourselves to their memories of trauma?

I have proposed that traumatic memory is invariably a half memory, for it is usually the case that an account of the person's response to the traumas of their history is not present in this memory. It has been erased – perhaps because these responses were ridiculed and diminished, or because these responses were not recognised and confirmed or acknowledged in a way that would contribute to them becoming more familiar to the person, and honoured by them. It is in this sense that I have described the significance of restoring traumatic memory to its fullness through the development of a rich account of how a person responded to the trauma they were subject to. These rich accounts include a broad and solid understanding about the foundations of these responses; that is, a broad and solid understanding of what these responses reflect about what the person has intended for their life, and what these responses reflect about what the person gives value to.

Could these sorts of inquiries take place within child protection work?

In consultations with young people who are the focus of child protection investigation, and with their parents and siblings, I believe it to be of vital importance that these consultations include very significant inquiry into the responses of these young people to what is perceived to be abusive and/or neglectful. Such consultations contribute to the development of a full account of the young person's experiences of trauma, one that will render them far less vulnerable to the diminution of their sense of personal agency. It will provide for them a foundation for the development of a sense of being able to intervene in one's life to shape one's existence, and this will be an antidote to experiences of impotence, emotional paralysis, of futility, and of personal desolation. Secondly, the further development of an account of the child's responses to what is perceived to be abusive or neglectful of them has the potential to significantly influence decisions about child protection action. These responses can be supported and further encouraged, and can form a foundation of safety for the young person.

Can you say more about the sorts of knowledge and skills of children who have endured abuse and neglect?

Many of children's responses to what is perceived to be abusive and/or neglectful are founded upon specific knowledges and skills. There are many categories of these knowledges and skills. One such category involves knowledges about and skill in relation to the creation of contexts of safety. Another involves knowledge about and skill in the care-taking of others. And so on.

If we create a context in which these skills and knowledges can be acknowledged, what then?

Once these skills and knowledges are drawn out, as well as some of the other knowledges and skills that children are routinely employing in life, it becomes possible to trace the history of the development of these. Very often this includes contributions from parents whose ability to parent is under question. Although this parent may have acted in ways that raise concerns about safety and that have precipitated child protection action, it is usually the case that these actions that have aroused concern do not speak to the totality of the child's experiences of these parents.

When the development of some of the child's knowledges of life and skills of living implicate parents whose actions are being questioned or whose suitability to parent is under question, the rich description of their contribution to these knowledges and skills can have a profound effect in shaping their parenting practices. This positive implication of parents can be taken up in therapeutic conversations that focus on the development and redevelopment of parenting practices that are not neglectful or abusive, and that will augment children's lives.

Of course, having said this, I acknowledge that there are occasions upon which abuse and neglect do represent the totality of a child's experience of a parent.

If these ways of implicating parents in the development of children's skills and knowledges contribute to changing parenting practices, then I can see how these fit within a child protection paradigm. Can I just ask you one more question about the extended consultations of children about their responses to abuse and neglect ... Are these relevant only to older children and young people?

I believe there are options in relation to extended consultations that are relevant to the consultation of both older and younger children from the age of four or five on. There are many ways of facilitating the consultation with young children, including through the use of 'stuffed colleagues', which is the subject of a chapter in this book. I will say that I have found the contribution of older siblings to be very helpful in the consultation of young children. In fact, I think there are options for extended consultation of children that are relevant in all contexts of child protection investigation, and that these consultations can have a significant effect on shaping subsequent child protection action. This is even the case in circumstances in which young people are in such peril that immediate and decisive action must be taken to remove them from contexts of abuse and neglect.

Well Michael, we have covered a lot of ground. I've really enjoyed this conversation and look forward to the next one!

Printed in Dunstable, United Kingdom

64175514R00087